AT HOME
with LYNN
CRAWFORD

AT HOME
with LYNN
CRAWFORD

200 OF MY FAVOURITE
EASY RECIPES

PENGUIN

an imprint of Penguin Canada Books Inc.

Published by the Penguin Group
Penguin Canada Books Inc., 90 Eglinton Avenue East, Suite 700,
Toronto, Ontario, Canada   M4P 2Y3

Penguin Group (USA) Inc., 375 Hudson Street, New York, New York 10014, U.S.A.
Penguin Books Ltd, 80 Strand, London WC2R 0RL, England
Penguin Ireland, 25 St Stephen's Green, Dublin 2, Ireland (a division of Penguin Books Ltd)
Penguin Group (Australia), 707 Collins Street, Melbourne, Victoria 3008, Australia (a division of Pearson Australia Group Pty Ltd)
Penguin Books India Pvt Ltd, 11 Community Centre, Panchsheel Park, New Delhi – 110 017, India
Penguin Group (NZ), 67 Apollo Drive, Rosedale, Auckland 0632, New Zealand (a division of Pearson New Zealand Ltd)
Penguin Books (South Africa) (Pty) Ltd, 24 Sturdee Avenue, Rosebank, Johannesburg 2196, South Africa

Penguin Books Ltd, Registered Offices: 80 Strand, London WC2R 0RL, England

First published 2013

2 3 4 5 6 7 8 9 10 (CR)

Copyright © Lynn Crawford, 2013

Food Photography: Kathleen Finlay
Prop and Food Stylist: Sasha Seymour
Food Stylist and Recipe Tester: Lora Kirk

Manufactured in the U.S.A.

Library and Archives Canada Cataloguing in Publication
Crawford, Lynn
At home with Lynn Crawford / Lynn Crawford.
Includes index.
ISBN 978-0-14-318706-6
1. Cooking. 2. Cookbooks. I. Title.
TX714.C68 2013   641.5   C2013-901341-5

Visit the Penguin Canada website at www.penguin.ca

Special and corporate bulk purchase rates available;
please see www.penguin.ca/corporatesales or call 1-800-810-3104, ext. 2477.

This cookbook is
for my mom

Also by Lynn Crawford

Lynn Crawford's Pitchin' In

{ CONTENTS }

{INTRODUCTION}

I've been cooking for years! I love what I do and can't imagine doing anything else. I love food so much, it's kind of a wonderful obsession. When I first started cooking I never imagined that it would totally take over my life, but in a good way! I wake up every morning and it's all about food and cooking, every day. What's wrong with that? Absolutely nothing!

I have worked at so many incredible restaurants and with so many wonderful, inspiring, and talented chefs who have always been driven to cook with all their heart and passion. I have always surrounded myself with people who love food. This is when I feel most at home. And, nothing beats cooking in my own home kitchen.

This cookbook is all about home. It's personal, fun, and filled with the people I've known, the places I've lived, worked, and visited, and of course, the food that I love to cook at home. I wanted to share some of my favorite recipes with you. I didn't want to over-complicate any of them. These are chef-inspired easy recipes, recipes that I regularly cook at home with influences from my mother and friends.

When I look back at my career, I'm amazed that I've learned so much. My love for food has taken me across the globe, and at each destination, with every experience, I have grown as a chef. I am very lucky to have had so many incredible experiences. I've included lots of recipes in this book that were inspired by my travels that I now love to cook at home

Food and cooking should be a fun and enjoyable occasion any time and any place! It's weekend brunches with friends, late night snacks and fancy cocktails, breakfasts that are more than just oatmeal, late lunches with a bottle of wine, dinner parties with lots of laughter, farmers' markets with too much to choose from, summer barbecues, winter stews and warm buttered biscuits, roast chicken with garlic and thyme, homemade jams, and butterscotch pudding.

Food and cooking is how I remember. It's names and faces, conversations and stories, the cities in which I've lived and visited, the seasons, the ingredients, the events. For me, all great memories are food memories, and my memories go back years. Peeling potatoes after school, Dad's Scottish breakfast on Christmas morning, Mom's split pea soup simmering on the stove, always a cup of tea after dinner, a road trip to find chocolate dipped ice cream cones and grape Mr. Mistys, lima beans hidden in glasses of milk, pizza parties, dinner parties and polishing silverware, just picked tomatoes sitting on the kitchen ledge, gravy sipped from a measuring cup, dinners made and shared with family, friends and friends' families. Beautiful food and always lots of laughter. It's so special to be able to celebrate these moments in this cookbook.

Food and cooking are about making and telling stories and what I'm most drawn to. Ingredients tell stories about land and local histories, farming, fishing, and harvesting. Recipes embellish these stories through tastes, smells, and presentations. It's so important for us all to be able to tell stories with and through food. I hope that this cookbook does all these things and also inspires you to do the same.

Most important, I want people to cook! Cook, eat, and share delicious food that's unpretentious and easy to make. For me food and cooking is all about sharing.

I hope you **enjoy** all of these recipes and just remember to keep on cooking with lots of heart and laughs!

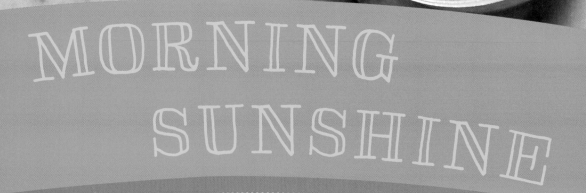

MORNING
SUNSHINE

SMOOTHIES & JUICES

Every morning I start my day with a smoothie or a glass of fresh juice. These recipes are **quick and easy** and will help make sure that you start the day off well.

Blazing Beet

Green Machine

Berry Blast

Pick Me Up

Berry Blast

Serves 1

· · · · · · · · ·

½ cup (125 mL) hulled strawberries

½ cup (125 mL) raspberries

1 banana

½ cup (125 mL) pomegranate juice

1 tbsp (15 mL) gingko powder

1 tbsp (15 mL) honey

4 ice cubes

· · · · · · · · ·

Combine all ingredients in a blender and process until smooth. Serve immediately.

Green Machine

Serves 1

· · · · · · · · ·

½ cucumber

2 celery stalks

1 cup (250 mL) fresh spinach

1 cup (250 mL) chopped kale

4 sprigs parsley

1 cup (250 mL) green grapes

· · · · · · · · ·

Using an electric juicer, process all ingredients into a glass. Stir to combine and serve immediately.

Pick Me Up

Serves 1

· · · · · · · · ·

1 carrot, peeled

1 wedge peeled pineapple

½ cup (125 mL) freshly squeezed orange juice

¼ tsp (1 mL) ground ginger

· · · · · · · · ·

Using an electric juicer, process all ingredients into a glass. Stir to combine and serve immediately.

Blazing Beet

Serves 1

· · · · · · · · ·

3 beets, with greens

1 pear

½ lemon

1½-inch (4 cm) piece fresh ginger

1 tsp (5 mL) chili powder

· · · · · · · · ·

Using an electric juicer, process all ingredients into a glass. Stir to combine and serve immediately.

HOMEMADE GRANOLA

Is there anything as nice as homemade granola? I know it might sound strange coming from someone who prefers savories over sweets, but I just love preparing it, smelling it as it cooks, eating it with thick yogurt and flavored honeys (page 13), and storing it in big glass jars. I love its texture the most. So have fun making your own.

Maple Cranberry Walnut Granola

Makes about 3 cups (750 mL)

· · · · · · · · · ·

2 cups (500 mL) old-fashioned rolled oats

½ cup (125 mL) sun-dried cranberries

¼ cup (60 mL) walnuts, toasted

¼ cup (60 mL) vegetable oil

3 tbsp (45 mL) honey

1 tbsp (15 mL) maple syrup

¾ tsp (4 mL) cinnamon

¾ tsp (4 mL) vanilla extract

½ tsp (2 mL) salt

· · · · · · · · · ·

Preheat oven to 325°F (160°C).

Combine oats, cranberries, and walnuts in a large bowl.

In a small saucepan, combine oil, honey, maple syrup, cinnamon, vanilla, and salt. Bring to a boil over medium heat, stirring constantly, then pour over oat mixture and stir to combine.

Spread granola on a parchment-lined baking sheet and bake, stirring once halfway through baking time, until crispy and toasted, about 20 minutes.

Let granola cool to room temperature before placing in an airtight container.

Chocolate Coconut Crunch Granola

Makes about 5 cups (1.25 L)

· · · · · · · · · ·

2 cups (500 mL) old-fashioned rolled oats

¾ cup (175 mL) sweetened flaked coconut

½ cup (125 mL) cocoa powder

¼ cup (60 mL) packed brown sugar

⅓ cup (75 mL) honey

¼ cup (60 mL) vegetable oil

½ tsp (2 mL) salt

¼ cup (60 mL) chocolate chips

½ cup (125 mL) banana chips

· · · · · · · · · ·

Preheat oven to 325°F (160°C).

In a large bowl, stir together oats and coconut.

In another bowl, stir together cocoa powder, sugar, honey, oil, and salt until combined, then pour over oat mixture and toss until evenly moistened.

Spread granola on a parchment-lined rimmed baking sheet and bake, stirring every 10 minutes, until crispy and toasted, about 30 minutes.

Let granola cool to room temperature before stirring in chocolate and banana chips and placing in an airtight container.

Vanilla & Tropical Fruit Granola

Makes about 4½ cups (1.125 L)

....

2 cups (500 mL) old-fashioned rolled oats
1 cup (250 mL) puffed rice cereal
¼ cup (60 mL) sweetened flaked coconut
¼ cup (60 mL) vegetable oil
¼ cup (60 mL) honey
¾ tsp (4 mL) cinnamon
¼ tsp (1 mL) salt
¼ tsp (1 mL) vanilla extract
¼ cup (60 mL) dried pineapple
¼ cup (60 mL) dried mango
¼ cup (60 mL) dried papaya
¼ cup (60 mL) macadamia nuts, toasted

....

Preheat oven to 325°F (160°C).

In a large bowl, stir together oats, rice cereal and coconut.

In another bowl, whisk together oil, honey, cinnamon, salt, and vanilla until combined, then pour over oat mixture and toss until evenly moistened.

Spread granola on a parchment-lined baking sheet and bake, stirring once about halfway through baking time, until crispy and toasted, about 15 minutes.

Let granola cool to room temperature before stirring in dried fruit and macadamia nuts and placing in an airtight container.

Ready-to-Go Granola Bars

Makes 12 bars

....

1 cup (250 mL) packed brown sugar
¾ cup (175 mL) peanut butter
½ cup (125 mL) corn syrup
1 stick (½ cup/125 mL) unsalted butter, melted
1 tbsp (15 mL) vanilla extract
3 cups (750 mL) old-fashioned rolled oats
1 cup (250 mL) mini chocolate chips
¾ cup (175 mL) sun-dried cranberries
½ cup (125 mL) sunflower seeds
¼ cup (60 mL) pumpkin seeds, toasted
¼ cup (60 mL) sesame seeds
¼ cup (60 mL) chopped pecans, toasted

....

Preheat oven to 375°F (190°C). Grease an 18- × 13-inch (46 × 32 cm) baking sheet and line with parchment paper.

In a large bowl, stir together sugar, peanut butter, corn syrup, butter, and vanilla until well combined.

In another large bowl, stir together oats, chocolate chips, cranberries, sunflower seeds, pumpkin seeds, sesame seeds, and pecans until combined, then pour over peanut butter mixture and knead with your hands until well combined.

Spread mixture evenly on baking sheet, cover with another piece of parchment paper, and use a rolling pin to compress mixture into a firm and uniform thickness.

Remove top piece of parchment paper from granola, then bake until golden, about 20 minutes. Let granola cool for 5 minutes before removing from pan, then let cool completely before cutting into 12 bars.

JAMS & JELLIES

Who doesn't like jams and jellies on toast or with pancakes and waffles, on muffins and cookies, on cakes, and swirled into ice cream? No one! Every summer you can find me up at the cottage picking strawberries and running to all the local farmers' markets collecting the best and sweetest fruits. **I love making and jarring up jams and jellies**, and the more hands in the kitchen, the better!

Maple Bourbon Peach Jam

Strawberry Honey Jam

Ginger Plum Jam

Blueberry Lemon Jam

Makes about 3 cups (750 mL)

· · · · · · · · ·

4 cups (1 L) blueberries
2 cups (500 mL) granulated sugar
Juice and grated zest of 2 lemons
2 envelopes (3 oz/85 mL each) liquid fruit pectin
    such as Certo

· · · · · · · · ·

In a large, heavy pot, combine blueberries, sugar, and lemon zest and juice. Bring to a boil over medium-high heat and cook for 5 minutes, stirring frequently. Skim off any foam.

Stir in liquid pectin and boil for 2 minutes longer. Remove from heat.

Ladle hot jam into sterilized jars, leaving ¼-inch (5 mm) headspace. Wipe jar rims and threads with a clean, damp cloth. Cover with lids and apply screw rings. Process jars in boiling water bath for 15 minutes. Remove the processed jars and let cool. Store in a cool, dark place.

Ginger Plum Jam

Makes about 3 cups (750 mL)

· · · · · · · · ·

4 cups (1 L) peeled pitted ripe plums cut
    in ½-inch (1 cm) cubes
2 cups (500 mL) brown sugar
1 tbsp (15 mL) grated fresh ginger
Grated zest and juice of 1 orange
1 envelope (3 oz/85 mL) liquid fruit pectin
    such as Certo

· · · · · · · · ·

In a large, heavy pot, combine plums, sugar, ginger, and orange juice and zest. Heat over medium-low heat, stirring until sugar has completely dissolved. Increase heat to medium-high and bring plum mixture to a boil. Cook for 10 minutes, stirring frequently. Skim off any foam.

Stir in liquid pectin and boil for 2 minutes longer. Remove from heat.

Ladle hot jam into sterilized jars, leaving ¼-inch (5 mm) headspace. Wipe jar rims and threads with a clean, damp cloth. Cover with lids and apply screw rings. Process jars in boiling water bath for 15 minutes. Remove the processed jars and let cool. Store in a cool, dark place.

Vanilla Grapefruit Marmalade

Makes about 2 cups (500 mL)

. . . .

2 large Ruby Red grapefruit, washed, halved, and seeded
2 cups (500 mL) granulated sugar
¼ cup (60 mL) grapefruit juice
1 vanilla bean, split lengthwise and seeds scraped out
1 tbsp (15 mL) lemon juice

. . . .

Cut grapefruit into ½-inch (1 cm) pieces. Place grapefruit in a large, heavy pot. Add enough water to cover and bring to a boil over medium-high heat. Cook for 2 minutes, then drain. Repeat process one more time.

In the same pot, combine grapefruit, sugar, grapefruit juice, and vanilla bean and seeds. Bring to a boil over medium heat and cook for 5 minutes, stirring frequently.

Reduce heat and simmer, stirring occasionally, until the fruit has softened, about 1 hour. Discard vanilla bean halves. Stir in lemon juice and remove from heat. Skim off any foam.

Ladle hot marmalade into sterilized jars, leaving ¼-inch (5 mm) headspace. Wipe jar rims and threads with a clean, damp cloth. Cover with lids and apply screw rings. Process jars in boiling water bath for 15 minutes. Remove the processed jars and let cool. Store in a cool, dark place.

Maple Bourbon Peach Jam

Makes about 2 cups (500 mL)

. . . .

4 cups (1 L) thinly sliced peeled pitted fresh peaches
  (or 21 oz/600 g frozen)
1 cup (250 mL) maple syrup
2 tbsp (30 mL) bourbon
1 vanilla bean, split lengthwise and seeds scraped out
1 tbsp (15 mL) lemon juice

. . . .

In a large, heavy pot, combine peaches, maple syrup, bourbon, and vanilla bean and seeds. Bring to a boil over medium heat and cook for 5 minutes, stirring frequently.

Reduce heat and simmer, stirring occasionally, until the fruit has softened, about 30 minutes. Skim off any foam. Discard vanilla bean halves.

Using a potato masher, gently crush peaches. Stir in lemon juice. Continue simmering until jam reaches desired consistency, about 10 minutes. Remove from heat.

Ladle hot jam into sterilized jars, leaving ¼-inch (5 mm) headspace. Wipe jar rims and threads with a clean, damp cloth. Cover with lids and apply screw rings. Process jars in boiling water bath for 15 minutes. Remove the processed jars and let cool. Store in a cool, dark place.

Strawberry Honey Jam

Makes about 4 cups (1 L)

....

5 cups (1.25 L) sliced strawberries
1 cup (250 mL) honey
3 envelopes (3 oz/85 mL each) liquid
  fruit pectin such as Certo
1 tbsp (15 mL) lemon juice

....

In a large, heavy pot, combine strawberries and honey. Bring to a boil over medium-high heat and cook for 5 minutes, stirring frequently. Skim off any foam.

Add liquid pectin and lemon juice. Boil for 1 minute longer. Remove from heat.

Ladle hot jam into sterilized jars, leaving ¼-inch (5 mm) headspace. Wipe jar rims and threads with a clean, damp cloth. Cover with lids and apply screw rings. Process jars in boiling water bath for 15 minutes. Remove the processed jars and let cool. Store in a cool, dark place.

Grape Jelly

Makes about 3 cups (750 mL)

....

2 cups (500 mL) unsweetened
  Concord grape juice
2 cups (500 mL) granulated sugar
2 envelopes (3 oz/85 mL each)
  liquid fruit pectin such as Certo

....

In a large, heavy pot, combine grape juice and sugar. Bring to a boil over medium heat and cook for 5 minutes, stirring frequently, until sugar has dissolved.

Stir in liquid pectin and cook for 1 minute. Remove from heat and skim off any foam.

Ladle hot jelly into sterilized jars, leaving ¼-inch (5 mm) headspace. Wipe jar rims and threads with a clean, damp cloth. Cover with lids and apply screw rings. Process jars in boiling water bath for 15 minutes. Remove the processed jars and let cool. Store in a cool, dark place.

BREAKFAST HONEYS

Honeys are so diverse, their tastes depending on where the bees pollinate, such as from orange blossoms, blueberry bushes, clover, buckwheat, or wild flowers. But it's also possible to flavor honey with flavoring agents. **It's simple to do at home.** I like to mix in fruits, nuts, herbs, or spices, but you can also experiment with different liquors. Use flavored honey as you would regular honey: in glazes and marinades, desserts, and baked goods, or to sweeten your tea. I especially love them with cheese, and at my restaurant, Ruby Watchco, we often serve flavored honey with our cheese course.

Vanilla Honey

Cinnamon Honey

Lemon Thyme Honey

Coffee Honey

Vanilla Honey

Makes 2 cups (500 mL)

. . . .

2 cups (500 mL) honey
1 vanilla bean, split lengthwise and seeds scraped out

. . . .

In a small saucepan, combine honey and vanilla bean and seeds. Bring to a simmer over medium heat, then pour mixture into a clean, sterilized jar. Cover and let sit to infuse for 24 hours before using.

Lemon Thyme Honey

Makes 2 cups (500 mL)

. . . .

1 lemon
2 cups (500 mL) honey
4 sprigs thyme

. . . .

Using a vegetable peeler, strip rind from lemon. Place in a small saucepan with honey and thyme, bring to a simmer over medium heat, then pour mixture into a clean, sterilized jar. Cover and let sit to infuse for 24 hours before using.

Cinnamon Honey

Makes 2 cups (500 mL)

. . . .

2 cups (500 mL) honey
2 cinnamon sticks

. . . .

In a small saucepan, combine honey and cinnamon sticks. Bring to a simmer over medium heat, then pour mixture into a clean, sterilized jar. Cover and let sit to infuse for 24 hours before using.

Coffee Honey

Makes 2 cups (500 mL)

. . . .

2 cups (500 mL) honey
1 tbsp (15 mL) very finely ground espresso beans

. . . .

In a small saucepan, combine honey and espresso. Bring to a simmer over medium heat, then pour mixture into a clean, sterilized jar. Cover and let sit to infuse for 24 hours before using.

Fruit & Nut Honey

Makes about 2 cups (500 mL)

. . . .

½ cup (125 mL) chopped mixed nuts, such as walnuts,
   almonds, pecans, toasted
1 cup (250 mL) honey
2 tbsp (30 mL) golden raisins
2 tbsp (30 mL) sun-dried cranberries

. . . .

Place nuts in a clean, sterilized jar.

In a small saucepan, combine honey, raisins, and cranberries. Bring to a simmer over medium heat, then pour over nut mixture in jar. Let cool completely. Cover.

Bacon Chive Butter

BREAKFAST BUTTERS

Maple Raisin Butter

Chocolate
Espresso Butter

Honey
Pistachio
Butter

Strawberry
Butter

Butters are a great way to experiment with flavors. From making your own butter to flavoring it, these are sure to impress. We make fresh butter at the restaurant to serve with our much-loved Cheddar biscuits. **Nothing can compete with fresh butter**—it's so simple, and the result is memorable. The process also produces buttermilk, which I use to make pancakes and baked goods and to thicken vinaigrettes—Buttermilk Pancakes (page 49), Apple Cider Doughnuts (page 31), and Buttermilk Basil Ranch Dressing (page 60).

Homemade Butter & Buttermilk

Makes about 2 cups (500 mL) butter
and 4 cups (1 L) buttermilk

. . . .

6 cups (1.5 L) heavy (35%) cream

. . . .

Pour cream into the bowl of a stand mixer fitted with the whisk attachment, then cover bowl opening and top part of the mixer with plastic wrap or splash guard to contain the splattering.

Beat cream at medium-high speed until it holds soft peaks, about 10 minutes, then increase speed to high and beat until cream separates into thick, pale-yellow butter and thin, liquid buttermilk, about 5 minutes more.

Strain mixture through a fine-mesh sieve into a large bowl. Place both the butter and buttermilk in separate airtight containers and refrigerate. Butter will keep for up to 1 week refrigerated or 1 month frozen. Buttermilk will keep for 1 week refrigerated.

Maple Raisin Butter

Makes about ½ cup (125 mL)

. . . .

1 stick (½ cup/125 mL) unsalted butter,
   at room temperature
2 tbsp (30 mL) maple syrup
2 tbsp (30 mL) golden raisins

. . . .

In a small bowl, stir together butter and maple syrup until blended, then fold in raisins.

Place butter in an airtight container and refrigerate. Use within 2 weeks.

Honey Pistachio Butter

Makes about ½ cup (125 mL)

1 stick (½ cup/125 mL) unsalted butter,
   at room temperature
2 tbsp (30 mL) honey
½ tsp (2 mL) vanilla extract
2 tbsp (30 mL) pistachios, toasted and finely chopped

In a small bowl, stir together butter, honey, and vanilla until blended, then fold in pistachios.

Place butter in an airtight container and refrigerate. Use within 2 weeks.

Chocolate Espresso Butter

Makes about ½ cup (125 mL)

2 tsp (10 mL) instant espresso powder
2 tsp (10 mL) cocoa powder
2 tsp (10 mL) water
½ tsp (2 mL) vanilla
1 stick (½ cup/125 mL) unsalted butter,
   at room temperature
2 tbsp (30 mL) icing sugar
1 tsp (5 mL) cinnamon

In a small bowl, stir together coffee powder, cocoa powder, water, and vanilla until well combined.

In another small bowl, cream together butter, icing sugar, and cinnamon until light and fluffy, then stir in coffee mixture and beat until smooth.

Place butter in an airtight container and refrigerate. Use within 1 month.

Bacon Chive Butter

Makes about ½ cup (125 mL)

2 slices bacon, cooked until crisp and finely chopped
1 stick (½ cup/125 mL) unsalted butter,
   at room temperature
¼ cup (60 mL) finely chopped chives
Salt and pepper

In a small bowl, stir together bacon, butter, and chives until combined, then season to taste with salt and pepper.

Place butter in an airtight container and refrigerate. Use within 2 weeks.

Strawberry Butter

Makes about 1½ cups (375 mL)

2 sticks (1 cup/250 mL) unsalted butter,
   at room temperature
3 tbsp (45 mL) honey
½ cup (125 mL) strawberries, hulled and thinly sliced
1 tsp (5 mL) vanilla extract

In a small bowl, stir together all ingredients until well combined.

Place butter in an airtight container and refrigerate. Use within 1 week.

BREAKFAST SPREADS

These spreads are **fun alternatives** to jams, jellies, and flavored butters. They're so versatile. Here are a few of my favorites, both sweet and savory. I like to make big batches so I have enough for the week. These spreads are not just for breakfast. I like to put them on eggs, have them with roasted veggies, or slather them over bagels or scones for afternoon tea.

Sweet Orange Mascarpone Spread

Makes about ¾ cup (175 mL)

....

½ cup (125 mL) mascarpone cheese
2 tbsp (30 mL) heavy (35%) cream
2 tbsp (30 mL) honey
Grated zest of 1 orange

....

In a small bowl, beat together all ingredients until smooth. Cover and refrigerate until ready to serve.

Smoked Salmon, Caper & Dill Spread

Makes about 2 cups (500 mL)

....

1 cup (250 mL) cream cheese, at room temperature
1 tbsp (15 mL) lemon juice
¾ cup (175 mL) smoked salmon, finely chopped
2 tbsp (30 mL) finely chopped dill
1 tbsp (15 mL) capers, finely chopped
Salt and pepper

....

In a small bowl, beat together cream cheese and lemon juice, then fold in salmon, dill, and capers. Season to taste with salt and pepper. Cover and refrigerate until ready to serve.

Bacon Cream Cheese Spread

Makes about 2 cups (500 mL)

....

1 lb (450 g) smoked bacon, diced
1 medium onion, finely chopped
2 cups (500 mL) cream cheese, softened
Cracked black pepper

....

In a large skillet over medium heat, cook bacon until fat has rendered and bacon is crisp, about 15 minutes. Using a slotted spoon, transfer bacon to paper towels to drain.

Remove all but 1 tbsp (15 mL) bacon fat from skillet. Add onions; sauté until tender, about 5 minutes. Transfer onions to a plate and cool slightly.

In a food processer, combine cream cheese, bacon, and onions; pulse to combine. Transfer mixture to a bowl and season to taste with pepper. Cover and refrigerate until ready to serve.

Peanut Butter Spread

Makes about 3 cups (750 mL)

....

2½ cups (625 mL) skinned unsalted peanuts, toasted
3 tbsp (45 mL) vegetable oil
3 tbsp (45 mL) honey

....

In a food processor, process peanuts until finely ground. Add oil and process until smooth.

With motor running, add honey and process until mixture tightens up and becomes semi-firm. Transfer to a bowl, cover, and refrigerate until ready to serve.

Apple Spread

Makes about 2 cups (500 mL)

· · · · · · · · · ·

2 lb (900 g) apples, peeled, quartered, and cut in 1-inch
  (2.5 cm) pieces
1 cup (250 mL) apple cider or apple juice
1 vanilla bean, split lengthwise and seeds scraped out
1 cup (250 mL) packed brown sugar
2 tbsp (30 mL) lemon juice
1 tsp (5 mL) cinnamon

· · · · · · · · · ·

In a large saucepan, combine apples and cider.
Bring to a boil over medium-high heat, stirring
occasionally, then reduce heat to low and simmer,
stirring occasionally, until apples are tender, about
25 minutes.

Stir in vanilla bean and seeds, sugar, lemon juice,
and cinnamon and continue cooking until the
mixture is very thick, about 30 minutes more.
Remove vanilla bean.

Place apple butter in an airtight container and
refrigerate. Use within 2 weeks.

Spiced Pear Spread

Makes about 4 cups (1 L)

· · · · · · · · · ·

2 lb (900 g) Bartlett pears, peeled, cored, and cut
  in 1-inch (2.5 cm) chunks
⅓ cup (75 mL) dry white wine
1 tbsp (15 mL) lemon juice
1 cup (250 mL) granulated sugar
4 whole cloves
1 vanilla bean, split lengthwise and seeds scraped out
1 cinnamon stick
¼ tsp (1 mL) ground cardamom
¼ tsp (1 mL) salt

· · · · · · · · · ·

In a large saucepan, stir together pears, wine, and
lemon juice. Simmer, covered, over medium-low
heat until pears are soft, about 20 minutes.

Transfer pear mixture to a food processor and
purée. Return purée to saucepan and stir in sugar,
cloves, vanilla bean and seeds, cinnamon stick,
cardamom, and salt. Cook over medium-low heat
until sugar has dissolved, about 5 minutes.

Increase heat to medium and boil gently, stirring
frequently, until mixture thickens and mounds
slightly on a spoon, about 30 minutes.

Discard cloves, vanilla bean, and cinnamon stick.
Pour mixture into a bowl, cover, and refrigerate
until ready to serve.

BREAKFAST BAKERY

I don't often prefer sweets to savories, but **I do love to bake**. There's something so relaxing about having to be precise, and baking is all about precision. That doesn't mean that you can't play around with recipes. In fact, I encourage you to! It's just critical to get the basics right, otherwise your hard work is often lost. Small mistakes have dramatic effects. Because baking can sometimes go quite wrong, it's hugely satisfying when you get the perfect result.

These recipes are not too difficult, but here are some tips and tricks.

- My Hot 'n' Sticky Buns (page 25) are traditional Chelsea buns. These are also wonderful filled with jams, jellies, or marmalades. I've tried them with the Ginger Plum Jam (page 9) and Vanilla Grapefruit Marmalade (page 10). Just spread it on the dough before rolling and baking.

- I always have too many bananas taking up precious space in my freezer. The Banana Nut Bread (page 26) is an easy way to make space for leftover lasagna and chicken soup, while at the same time becoming popular with family and friends. However impatient you are—and it's difficult not to be with the beautiful smells filling the kitchen—let the loaf cool before removing it from the pan, otherwise you risk getting an uneven, crumbled exterior.

- The Apple Muffins (page 27) are made extra-moist by the diced apples. So don't worry if your dough at first seems a little dry; the apples release their juices while baking. These also taste great with the Streusel-Nut Topping (page 27), which I sprinkle on top before baking.

- The Cheddar Jalapeño Biscuits (page 29) are similar to the ones that I serve at the restaurant. I've added the jalapeños for heat and made it more cornbread-like than proper biscuit. The cornmeal makes the dough more textured.

- The trick to getting wonderful little layers in the Cranberry Scones (page 30) is to use chilled butter so that the glutens in the dough don't become too dense. For this same reason, don't overdo it on the mixing. Just be cool!

- While the Apple Cider Doughnuts (page 31) might seem intimidating at first, don't let that stop you! These beauties are so worth it, and are not as challenging as you think. Just make sure that your oil is at the right temperature, and don't get distracted.

Hot 'n' Sticky Buns

Makes 12 buns

. . . .

½ cup (125 mL) warm water mixed with a pinch of granulated sugar

1 tbsp (15 mL) active dry yeast

3 cups (750 mL) warm milk

1¼ cups (300 mL) unsalted butter, melted

½ cup (125 mL) plus 4 tsp (20 mL) granulated sugar

½ tsp (2 mL) salt

6 large eggs

12 cups (2.8 L) all-purpose flour

4 tsp (20 mL) cinnamon

. . . .

In a small bowl, combine warm water with yeast. Let stand until foamy, about 8 minutes.

Meanwhile, in the bowl of a stand mixer fitted with the paddle attachment, beat together milk, 1 cup (250 mL) of the melted butter, ½ cup (125 mL) of the sugar, salt, and eggs until well combined. Beat in yeast mixture, then beat in flour, scraping down sides of bowl, until a soft, sticky dough forms.

On a floured work surface, knead dough until smooth and elastic, about 8 minutes, adding additional flour to work surface, if necessary, to prevent dough from sticking.

Turn dough into a greased bowl, cover with plastic wrap, and let rise in a warm spot until doubled in size, about 2½ hours.

Punch down dough, then roll out on a floured work surface to a 12- × 9-inch (30 × 23 cm) rectangle. Brush off excess flour, then brush surface of dough with remaining ¼ cup (60 mL) melted butter.

Combine remaining 4 tsp (20 mL) sugar with cinnamon and sprinkle over surface of dough.

Starting at one long side, tightly roll dough into a log, then cut crosswise into 12 rounds. Place rounds cut side up and 1 inch (2.5 cm) apart in a greased 13- × 9-inch (3 L) baking dish or cake pan. Cover buns with plastic wrap and let rise in a warm spot until almost doubled in size, about 1 hour.

Meanwhile, preheat oven to 375°F (190°C).

Bake buns until deep golden brown, about 30 minutes. Run a small knife around pan sides to loosen buns and let cool for 30 minutes before serving.

Banana Nut Bread

Makes 16 servings

· · · · · · · · ·

2 cups (500 mL) all-purpose flour
1½ tsp (7 mL) baking powder
½ tsp (2 mL) baking soda
½ tsp (2 mL) cinnamon
¼ tsp (1 mL) nutmeg
¼ tsp (1 mL) salt
⅛ tsp (0.5 mL) ground ginger
2 large eggs
1½ cups (375 mL) mashed bananas
1 cup (250 mL) granulated sugar
½ cup (125 mL) vegetable oil
¼ cup (60 mL) chopped walnuts
Streusel-Nut Topping (recipe on facing page)

· · · · · · · · ·

Preheat oven to 350°F (180°C).

In a large bowl, stir together flour, baking powder, baking soda, cinnamon, nutmeg, salt, and ginger.

In another bowl, lightly beat eggs. Add bananas, sugar, and oil; stir until sugar has dissolved. Stir wet ingredients into flour mixture just until moistened. Fold in walnuts. Spoon batter into a greased 9- × 5-inch (2 L) loaf pan and sprinkle with streusel-nut topping.

Bake until a toothpick inserted in the center of the loaf comes out clean, about 55 minutes. To prevent overbrowning, if necessary cover top of loaf loosely with foil during the last 15 minutes of baking time.

Let cool on a rack for 10 minutes before removing loaf from pan, then cool completely before slicing.

Apple Muffins

Makes 12 muffins

. . . .

1 cup (250 mL) all-purpose flour

1 cup (250 mL) whole wheat pastry flour

2 tsp (10 mL) baking powder

1 tsp (5 mL) salt

2 large eggs

1 cup (250 mL) milk

1 stick (½ cup/125 mL) unsalted butter, melted

½ cup (125 mL) granulated sugar

¼ cup (60 mL) packed brown sugar

2 tsp (10 mL) cinnamon

2 apples, cored and finely diced

. . . .

Preheat oven to 350°F (180°C). Generously grease a 12-cup muffin pan.

In a medium bowl, sift together all-purpose flour, whole wheat pastry flour, baking powder, and salt.

In a large bowl, lightly beat eggs. Add milk, butter, eggs, granulated and brown sugars, and cinnamon; whisk until sugars have dissolved, then fold in apples. Fold flour mixture into wet ingredients just until combined. Divide batter among muffin cups.

Bake until a toothpick inserted in center of muffins comes out clean, about 25 minutes. Let cool on a rack for 5 minutes before removing muffins, then cool to room temperature before serving.

Streusel-Nut Topping

Makes about 1 cup (250 mL)

. . . .

3 tbsp (45 mL) packed brown sugar

2 tbsp (30 mL) all-purpose flour

4 tsp (20 mL) cold unsalted butter

¼ cup (60 mL) chopped walnuts

. . . .

In a small bowl, combine sugar and flour. Using a pastry blender, cut in butter until mixture resembles coarse crumbs. Stir in chopped walnuts.

Cheddar Jalapeño Biscuits

Makes 12 biscuits

....

1½ cups (375 mL) all-purpose flour

¾ cup (175 mL) stone-ground cornmeal

1 tbsp (15 mL) baking powder

1 tbsp (15 mL) granulated sugar

1 tsp (5 mL) kosher salt

1¼ cups (300 mL) shredded sharp Cheddar cheese

¼ cup (60 mL) chopped chives

2 tbsp chopped pickled jalapeños

1 large egg

1 cup (250 mL) milk

¼ cup (60 mL) canola oil

....

Preheat oven to 400°F (200°C).

In a medium bowl, stir together flour, cornmeal, baking powder, sugar, and salt. Stir in the cheese, chives, and the jalapeños.

In another bowl, lightly beat egg, then whisk in milk and oil. Fold into flour mixture just until combined.

Turn out onto a floured surface and gently knead for 1 minute. Roll out into a 8- × 12-inch (20 × 30 cm) rectangle about 1 inch (2.5 cm) thick. Cut into 12 pieces. Transfer biscuits to an ungreased baking sheet. Brush with egg wash. Bake until golden brown, about 20 minutes. Serve warm.

Cranberry Scones

Makes 8 scones

. . . .

2 cups (500 mL) all-purpose flour

⅓ cup (75 mL) granulated sugar

1 tbsp (15 mL) baking powder

½ tsp (2 mL) salt

6 tbsp (90 mL) chilled unsalted butter, cut in small pieces

⅓ cup (150 mL) heavy (35%) cream

½ cup (125 mL) sun-dried cranberries, finely chopped

. . . .

Preheat oven to 425°F (220°C).

In a medium bowl, whisk together flour, sugar, baking powder, and salt. Cut in butter with a pastry blender or two knives until mixture resembles coarse crumbs.

Stir in cream just until moistened, then gently fold in cranberries.

On a lightly floured work surface, knead dough gently until it comes together in a ball, about 5 minutes. Roll out into a disc 1 inch (2.5 cm) thick and cut into 8 wedges.

Place scones 2 inches (5 cm) apart on a baking sheet. If desired, brush tops with egg wash and sprinkle with granulated sugar.

Bake until golden brown, about 12 minutes. Transfer to a rack to cool.

Apple Cider Doughnuts

Makes about 12 doughnuts

· · · · · · · · ·

1 cup (250 mL) apple cider

3½ cups (875 mL) all-purpose flour

2 tsp (10 mL) baking powder

1 tsp (5 mL) baking soda

½ tsp (2 mL) cinnamon

½ tsp (2 mL) salt

4 tbsp (60 mL) unsalted butter, at room temperature

1 cup (250 mL) granulated sugar

2 large eggs

½ cup (125 mL) buttermilk

1 cup (250 mL) granulated sugar mixed with 2 tbsp (30 mL) cinnamon, for dusting

Vegetable oil, for deep-frying

· · · · · · · · ·

In a small pot over low heat, reduce apple cider to ¼ cup (60 mL). Set aside.

In a medium bowl, stir together flour, baking powder, baking soda, cinnamon, and salt.

In the bowl of a stand mixer fitted with the paddle attachment, cream butter with 1 cup (250 mL) granulated sugar at medium speed until light and fluffy, about 3 minutes. Add eggs, 1 at a time, beating after each addition until combined. Scrape down sides of bowl.

Reduce mixer speed to low and gradually beat in reduced apple cider and buttermilk, mixing just until well combined. Spoon in flour mixture and continue mixing until dough comes together.

Turn dough out onto a floured work surface and roll to a uniform ½-inch (1 cm) thickness with a floured rolling pin. Use more flour, if needed, to prevent dough from sticking. Transfer dough to a parchment-lined baking sheet and set in the freezer to harden slightly, about 20 minutes.

With a 3-inch (8 cm) doughnut cutter, punch out doughnuts. Place cut doughnuts and doughnut holes on a second parchment-lined baking sheet and refrigerate for 30 minutes.

Meanwhile, in a large, deep saucepan, heat 3 inches (8 cm) of oil to 350°F (180°C). Place cinnamon-sugar mixture in a small, shallow bowl.

Working in batches, add a few doughnuts at a time to the oil, being careful not to crowd the pan, and fry until golden brown, about 60 seconds per side, turning doughnuts only once. With a slotted spoon, transfer cooked doughnuts to paper towels to drain, then immediately dip into cinnamon sugar.

Doughnuts are best served while still warm.

BREAKFAST & BRUNCH

I love Sunday brunch. I love its casualness, its inclusiveness, its anything-goes atmosphere. I believe that **people are happiest at brunch**. It's the weekend, you snuck another hour in bed, and once up and ready to go, you can start to cook up some of my favorite brunch recipes and share with your family and friends. No matter who you spend brunch with, these recipes will help keep it fun and delicious!

Green Eggs & Ham

I'm very literal, so when I read Dr. Seuss's *Green Eggs and Ham*, I knew I needed those technicolor eggs. Here's something fantastical and fun for you "fictional" food lovers. *Serves 4*

2 cups (500 mL) packed baby spinach
2 tbsp (30 mL) grated Parmesan cheese
¼ cup (60 mL) olive oil
8 large eggs
½ tsp (2 mL) salt
¼ tsp (1 mL) black pepper
2 tbsp (30 mL) butter
4 slices crispy prosciutto (page 65)

In a food processor, combine spinach and Parmesan; pulse to combine. With motor running, slowly add oil and continue to process until smooth.

Whisk together eggs, ¼ cup (60 mL) spinach mixture, salt, and pepper.

In a large nonstick skillet over medium heat, melt butter. Pour in egg mixture and cook, stirring gently, until just barely set, about 5 minutes.

Crumble prosciutto over eggs and serve immediately.

Cuddled Eggs Three Ways

Yes, cuddled, not coddled. The eggs are like edible duvets for the wonderful ingredients inside: the leek and artichoke, black beans and pickled jalapeños, romesco sauce and cherry tomatoes. These little egg dishes are packed with flavor, satisfying, and so easy to prepare.

Eggs Française with Leek & Artichokes

Serves 2

1 tbsp (15 mL) butter

1 tbsp (15 mL) olive oil

1 leek, white part only, cut in ¼-inch (5 mm) slices

4 small baby artichokes, quartered

¼ cup (60 mL) water

1 cup (250 mL) heavy (35%) cream

½ cup (125 mL) finely grated Parmesan cheese

Grated zest of 1 lemon

Salt and pepper

2 eggs

¼ cup (60 mL) chopped parsley

Fresh baguette

Preheat oven to 375°F (190°C). Grease 2 individual baking dishes.

In a medium saucepan over medium heat, melt butter, then add oil. Add leek and artichokes; sauté for 3 minutes. Add water, cover, and cook until vegetables are fork-tender, about 7 minutes.

Stir in cream, bring to a boil, and cook, stirring frequently, until liquid has reduced by half.

Add Parmesan and lemon zest; stir until cheese has melted. Remove mixture from heat and season to taste with salt and pepper.

With a slotted spoon, remove leeks and artichokes from cream mixture and divide between baking dishes, leaving room in the middle of each dish for the egg. Crack an egg into center of each dish. Spoon cream mixture over leeks and artichokes (but not eggs).

Bake until egg whites have just set, about 15 minutes. Garnish with parsley and serve immediately with sliced baguette.

South of
the Border Eggs

Opa! Eggs

Eggs Française

Opa! Eggs
Serves 2

....

1 cup (250 mL) Romesco Sauce (page 172)
½ cup (125 mL) cherry tomatoes, halved
2 tsp (10 mL) coarsely chopped dill
Salt and pepper
2 eggs
¼ cup (60 mL) crumbled feta cheese
Pita slices, toasted

....

Preheat oven to 375°F (190°C). Grease 2 individual baking dishes.

In a small saucepan, combine romesco sauce, tomatoes, and dill; season to taste with salt and pepper. Bring to a boil over medium-high heat.

Divide mixture between baking dishes. Crack an egg into center of each dish. Top with cheese.

Bake until egg whites have just set, about 15 minutes. Serve immediately with toasted sliced pita.

South of the Border Eggs

Serves 2

....

1 tbsp (15 mL) olive oil

½ cup (125 mL) finely chopped red onion

2 cloves garlic, minced

½ cup (125 mL) finely diced yellow bell pepper

½ tsp (2 mL) ground cumin

1 can (19 oz/540 mL) black beans, drained and rinsed

½ cup (125 mL) chicken stock

1 tbsp (15 mL) finely chopped pickled jalapeño
  peppers (page 67)

Salt and pepper

2 eggs

1 lime, quartered

1 small avocado, peeled and cut in wedges

A few sprigs of cilantro

¼ cup (60 mL) sour cream

Hot sauce (optional)

2 cups (500 mL) tortilla chips

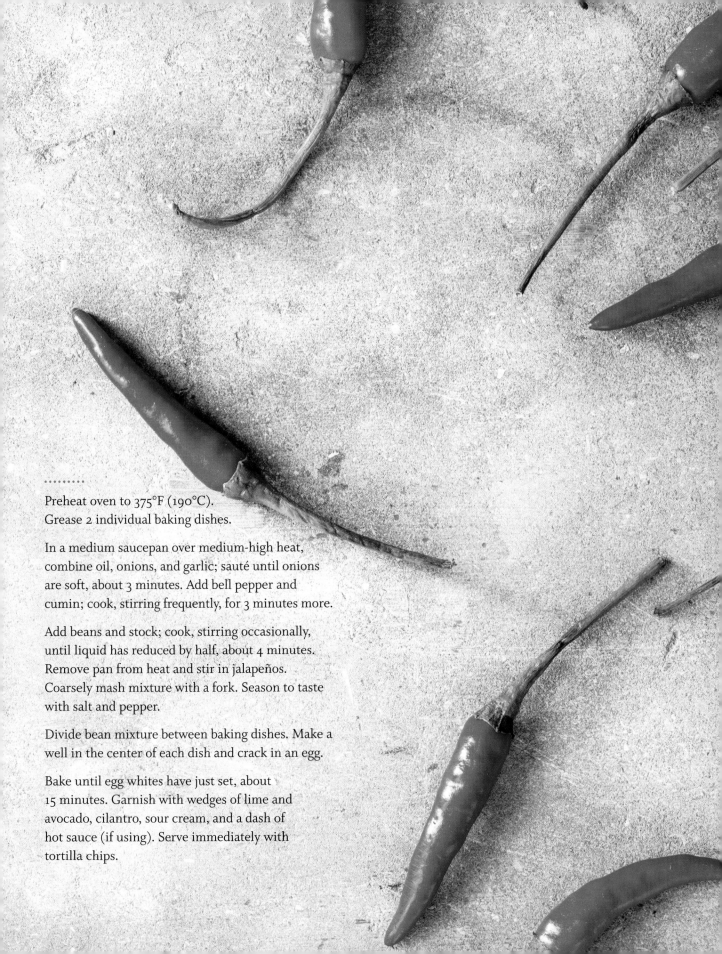

Preheat oven to 375°F (190°C).
Grease 2 individual baking dishes.

In a medium saucepan over medium-high heat,
combine oil, onions, and garlic; sauté until onions
are soft, about 3 minutes. Add bell pepper and
cumin; cook, stirring frequently, for 3 minutes more.

Add beans and stock; cook, stirring occasionally,
until liquid has reduced by half, about 4 minutes.
Remove pan from heat and stir in jalapeños.
Coarsely mash mixture with a fork. Season to taste
with salt and pepper.

Divide bean mixture between baking dishes. Make a
well in the center of each dish and crack in an egg.

Bake until egg whites have just set, about
15 minutes. Garnish with wedges of lime and
avocado, cilantro, sour cream, and a dash of
hot sauce (if using). Serve immediately with
tortilla chips.

Sausage & Egg Bake

This dish is the inelegant marriage between Bangers and Mash and Bread Pudding. It doesn't require much work or finesse, but is it ever scrumptious. I've been known to whip this recipe up after a late night.

Serves 6

6 cups (1.5 L) bread cut in 1-inch (2.5 cm) cubes (about ½ large baguette)
6 cooked pork breakfast sausages
1 cup (250 mL) sautéed sliced mushrooms
1 cup (250 mL) sautéed baby spinach
¾ cup (175 mL) shredded Cheddar cheese
6 eggs
2 cups (500 mL) heavy (35%) cream
½ tsp (2 mL) salt
¼ tsp (1 mL) pepper

Preheat oven to 350°F (180°C).

Place bread cubes in a single layer in a greased 11- × 7-inch (2 L) glass baking dish. Arrange sausages, mushrooms, spinach, and Cheddar on top.

Whisk together eggs, cream, salt, and pepper. Pour over bread mixture and let rest for 15 minutes to allow egg mixture to soak into bread cubes.

Bake until a knife inserted in the center comes out clean, about 35 minutes. Cool on a rack for 5 minutes before cutting into squares and serving.

Croque Madame

....

If you can't have Paris, and you're craving something savory and substantial, then look no further than the reliable croque madame. Its fried egg hat makes it distinct from its culinary companion, the croque monsieur. This wonderful breakfast or brunch dish is luxurious, combining Gruyère cheese with more Gruyère cheese in the sophisticated Mornay sauce. This dish is hard to top! *Serves 4*

....

8 slices sourdough bread, ¾ inch (2 cm) thick
2 tbsp (30 mL) Dijon mustard
2 cups (500 mL) shredded Gruyère cheese
1 lb (450 g) sliced Montreal smoked meat

4 tbsp (60 mL) butter, at room temperature
1 cup (250 mL) warm Mornay sauce
   (recipe follows)
4 large eggs

....

Preheat broiler.

Spread 4 slices of bread with mustard. Top each slice with ¼ cup (60 mL) cheese. Divide smoked meat among slices and sprinkle each with ¼ cup (60 mL) remaining cheese. Top with remaining bread slices. Butter both sides of each sandwich.

Set a large skillet over medium heat. Working in two batches, cook sandwiches until golden and crisp, about 6 minutes per side. Transfer sandwiches to a small baking sheet.

Spoon ¼ cup (60 mL) Mornay sauce over each sandwich. Broil until brown, about 2 minutes.

Top each sandwich with a sunny-side-up fried egg and serve immediately.

Mornay Sauce
Makes about 1 cup (250 mL)

....

4 tsp (20 mL) butter
4 tsp (20 mL) all-purpose flour
1 cup (250 mL) milk
½ cup (125 mL) heavy (35%) cream

¼ cup (60 mL) shredded Gruyère cheese
Pinch of freshly grated nutmeg
Salt and pepper

....

In a medium saucepan over medium heat, melt butter. Sprinkle in flour and cook for 3 minutes, stirring constantly.

Whisk in milk and cream. Cook, stirring frequently, until sauce is thick enough to coat the back of a spoon, about 7 minutes. Remove pan from heat and stir in cheese and nutmeg. Season to taste with salt and pepper and keep warm until ready to use.

Spicy Chorizo & Potato Frittata with Pepper Jack Cheese

I think that frittatas are fantastic, simple, and versatile. This is my favorite frittata recipe. It has chorizo, potatoes, and cheese. It's rustic and wonderful for sharing. *Serves 4*

8 large eggs
½ cup (125 mL) heavy (35%) cream
½ tsp (2 mL) salt
¼ tsp (1 mL) pepper
2 tbsp (30 mL) olive oil
2 fresh spicy chorizo sausages, casings removed
½ cup (125 mL) thinly sliced red onion
1 medium Yukon Gold potato, thinly sliced
1 cup (250 mL) shredded pepper Jack cheese

Preheat oven to 375°F (190°C).

In a medium bowl, whisk together eggs and cream; season to taste with salt and pepper. Set aside.

In an ovenproof skillet over medium-high heat, add oil and sausage. Cook until sausage has browned, about 3 minutes, using a wooden spoon to break meat apart.

Add onions and potato and continue cooking, stirring constantly so potatoes don't stick, until potato slices are fork-tender, about 5 minutes.

Remove skillet from heat. Pour in reserved egg mixture and sprinkle cheese on top. Place skillet in oven and bake until cheese has melted and the tip of a knife inserted in center of frittata comes out clean, about 20 minutes. Let rest for 5 minutes before serving.

Boozy Baked French Toast with Almonds

·········

This is an all-in-one dish: French toast and Sunday coffee (with Baileys)—though you'll still need to take the coffee on the side. The brioche is extra-absorbent and has its own distinct sweet flavor, but feel free to use any of your favorite breakfast breads. My Hot 'n' Sticky Buns (page 25) work really well too. *Serves 6 to 8*

·········

1 loaf brioche or egg bread, cut in ½-inch (1 cm) cubes (8 cups/2 L)
4 large eggs
1¼ cups (300 mL) milk
½ cup (125 mL) Baileys liqueur
¼ cup (60 mL) granulated sugar
2 tsp (10 mL) vanilla extract
½ cup (125 mL) chopped toasted almonds

·········

Preheat oven to 350°F (180°C).

Spread bread cubes in a well-greased 13- × 9-inch (3 L) glass baking dish.

In a large bowl, whisk together eggs, milk, liqueur, sugar, and vanilla. Pour over bread cubes and press down gently to allow bread to soak up egg mixture. Sprinkle evenly with almonds.

Bake until golden brown, about 25 minutes. Serve warm with maple syrup.

Buttermilk Pancakes & Syrups

Enjoy these pancakes with one or two or more flavored syrups. Syrups are simple to make, and like jams and jellies, can be used in and on so many different dishes. They're great drizzled generously over these amazingly fluffy pancakes. Pile them high, pick your syrup, and dig in.

Makes six 5-inch (12 cm) pancakes

1¼ cups (300 mL) all-purpose flour
3 tbsp (45 mL) granulated sugar
2½ tsp (12 mL) baking powder
½ tsp (2 mL) salt
1 large egg
1¼ cups (300 mL) buttermilk
3 tbsp (45 mL) butter, melted
1 tsp (5 mL) vanilla extract

Preheat oven to 200°F (100°C).

In a medium bowl, whisk together flour, sugar, baking powder, and salt.

In a separate bowl, lightly beat egg. Whisk in buttermilk, melted butter, and vanilla. Pour over flour mixture and whisk just until combined.

Grease a large nonstick skillet and set over medium heat. Ladle in a scant ½ cup (125 mL) batter per pancake and cook, turning once, until golden, about 2 minutes per side. Transfer pancakes to a baking sheet and keep warm in oven. Repeat with remaining batter. Serve hot, topped with butter and maple syrup or flavored syrups.

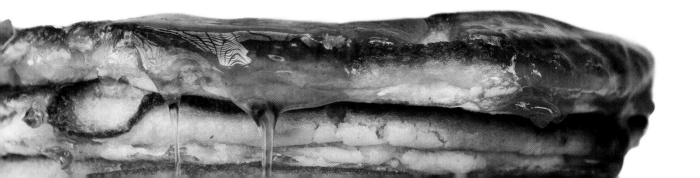

FLAVORED SYRUPS

Peanut Butter Syrup

Makes about 2 cups (500 mL)

....

1 cup (250 mL) maple syrup
½ cup (125 mL) water
3 tbsp (45 mL) butter
⅓ cup (75 mL) creamy or chunky peanut butter

....

Stir together maple syrup and water until combined. Set aside.

In a medium saucepan over low heat, melt butter. Add peanut butter and stir until thoroughly combined. Increase heat to medium-high, stir in reserved syrup mixture, and bring to a boil, stirring constantly. Reduce heat to low and simmer until mixture has thickened slightly, about 5 minutes.

Serve warm or cover and refrigerate; use within 1 week.

Cranberry Syrup

Makes about 2 cups (500 mL)

....

2 cups (500 mL) pure cranberry juice
1 cup (250 mL) fresh cranberries
¾ cup (175 mL) light corn syrup
¼ cup (60 mL) granulated sugar

....

In a medium saucepan, combine all ingredients. Cook over medium-high heat until sugar has dissolved and mixture comes to a rolling boil. Reduce heat to medium and continue cooking until mixture has reduced to about 2½ cups (625 mL).

Strain mixture through a fine-mesh sieve set over a bowl. Discard cranberry pulp. Pour syrup into an airtight container and refrigerate; use within 1 week.

Strawberry Syrup

Makes about 1½ cups (375 mL)

....

1 cup (250 mL) granulated sugar
1 cup (250 mL) water
2 cups (500 mL) strawberries, hulled and quartered

In a medium saucepan, combine sugar and water. Cook over medium-high heat until sugar has dissolved, then stir in strawberries. Bring to a boil.

Boil for 10 minutes, stirring constantly, then reduce heat to medium-low and simmer until strawberries are mushy and sauce has thickened, about 10 minutes more.

Strain mixture through a fine-mesh sieve set over a bowl. Discard strawberry pulp. Pour syrup into an airtight container and refrigerate; use within 1 week.

Maple Bacon Syrup

Makes about 1½ cups (375 mL)

....

¼ lb (115 g) applewood-smoked bacon, diced
1 cup (250 mL) maple syrup
2 sticks (1 cup/250 mL) unsalted butter, cut in pieces, at room temperature

....

In a small saucepan over medium heat, cook bacon, stirring frequently, just until crispy, about 5 minutes. Stir in maple syrup. When mixture starts to bubble, remove pan from heat and whisk in butter.

Pour syrup into an airtight container and refrigerate; use within 1 week. Serve at room temperature.

Blueberry Syrup

Makes 1 cup (250 mL)

....

2 cups (500 mL) fresh or frozen blueberries
1 cup (250 mL) maple syrup
2 tsp (10 mL) lemon juice

....

In a medium saucepan, combine all ingredients. Bring to a boil over medium-high heat, then reduce heat to low and simmer, stirring occasionally, until blueberries are very soft. Remove pan from heat and, using a potato masher, mash blueberries.

Strain mixture through a fine-mesh sieve set over a bowl. Discard blueberry pulp. Pour syrup into an airtight container and refrigerate; use within 1 week.

Lemon Ricotta Hotcakes
with Blueberry Syrup

Ricotta is a sweet, moist, wonderful soft-grained cheese. I love using it in all sorts of dishes, especially in these wonderful hotcakes. The ricotta gives them an inviting cheesecake-like taste and texture. And for the record, I have made over a million of these! *Serves 4*

3 large eggs plus 2 large egg whites
1 cup (250 mL) smooth ricotta cheese
¼ cup (60 mL) butter, melted
2 tbsp (30 mL) granulated sugar
1 tbsp (15 mL) grated lemon zest
¼ tsp (1 mL) salt
1½ cups (375 mL) all-purpose flour
Blueberry Syrup (page 51)

In a medium bowl, whisk together whole eggs, ricotta, butter, sugar, lemon zest, and salt until smooth. Stir in flour just until combined.

In another bowl, whisk egg whites until stiff peaks form. Using a spatula, gently fold whites into batter until well combined.

Set a greased, large nonstick skillet over medium heat. Drop in heaping tablespoons of batter to form small, round hotcakes. Cook until golden, about 1½ minutes per side. Serve hotcakes warm with blueberry syrup.

Tattie Scones

This recipe conjures so many wonderful memories, so many Christmas mornings with my dad's traditional Scottish breakfast, which included tattie scones, fried eggs, back bacon, baked beans, black pudding, and dark coffee. The tattie scones were integral. They're salty and crispy with warm, soft centers. These are best made with leftover potatoes from the night before. *Makes 8 scones*

....

2 cups (500 mL) warm Whipped Potatoes (page 198)
¼ cup (60 mL) butter, softened
1 cup (250 mL) all-purpose flour
1 tsp (5 mL) salt
½ tsp (2 mL) baking powder
2 tbsp (30 mL) unsalted butter

....

Preheat oven to 200°F (100°C).

Stir together warm potatoes and softened butter until well combined.

In another bowl, stir together flour, salt, and baking powder, then stir into potato mixture just until combined.

Turn mixture out onto a lightly floured work surface and form into a ball. Cover with a tea towel and let rest until cooled to room temperature, about 20 minutes.

On a lightly floured work surface, roll out dough to 10- × 8-inch (25 × 20 cm) rectangle. Cut into 4 rectangles, then cut each rectangle diagonally into 2 wedges.

In a large skillet over medium heat, melt 1 tbsp (15 mL) unsalted butter. When foam subsides, add half of the scones and cook, turning once, until golden brown, about 7 minutes per side. Transfer scones to a baking sheet and keep warm in oven. Repeat with remaining butter and scones.

Bananas Foster Pancakes with Caramel Sauce

For those craving dessert before noon, here you go. But what's not to love about caramelized bananas? The aroma is intoxicating, and the flavor is just as mind-blowing. I dare you to resist this dish once you smell the bananas simmering in the hot, sweet caramel. *Makes six 5-inch (12 cm) pancakes*

....

1 large egg
2¼ cups (550 mL) milk
3 tbsp (45 mL) butter, melted
2 cups (500 mL) all-purpose flour
1 tbsp (15 mL) granulated sugar
4 tsp (20 mL) baking powder
½ tsp (2 mL) kosher salt
¼ cup (60 mL) unsalted butter
½ cup (125 mL) packed dark brown sugar
1 tbsp (15 mL) dark rum
1 tsp (5 mL) vanilla extract
2 bananas, cut in ½-inch (1 cm) slices

....

Preheat oven to 200°F (100°C).

In a large bowl, lightly beat egg. Whisk in milk and melted butter.

In a separate bowl, whisk together flour, sugar, baking powder, and salt. Add to egg mixture and whisk just until combined.

In a medium skillet over medium heat, melt ¼ cup (60 mL) unsalted butter. Stir in brown sugar and cook, stirring occasionally, until sugar has completely dissolved, about 5 minutes. Stir in rum and vanilla. Add banana slices in a single layer and cook, turning once, until bananas are caramelized, about 1 minute per side. Keep warm until ready to serve.

Grease a large nonstick skillet and set over medium heat. Ladle in ½ cup (125 mL) batter for each pancake and cook, turning once, until golden, about 2 minutes per side. Transfer pancakes to a baking sheet and keep warm in oven. Repeat with remaining batter.

Spoon banana mixture over hot pancakes and serve immediately.

IN A BOWL

DRESSINGS & VINAIGRETTES

Salad dressings are all about balance.
The best way to make an awesome dressing is
to experiment with different kinds of oils and
acids, two essential components. There are many
different kinds of each. The oil can be vegetable,
olive, peanut, sesame, or fats rendered from
meats. The acid can be vinegar or citrus juice, or
some combination of the two. I always tell cooks
not to be timid with the acid. It shouldn't be an
afterthought—it's in fact crucial to the salad's
overall flavor. So play around with different acids,
like sherry, champagne, and wine vinegars or
lemon, lime, and orange juice. For something
exciting, use Meyer lemons, which are as sweet as
they are tart.

Once you've perfected oils and acids, move on to
flavoring your dressings. This is the fun part, so be
creative. Use nuts, condiments, spices, or cheeses.
Experiment with the texture as well. **I love
dressings with some crunch.**

Brown Derby Vinaigrette

Makes about 2 cups (500 mL)

½ cup (125 mL) red wine vinegar
2 tsp (10 mL) balsamic vinegar
2 tbsp (30 mL) honey
2 tbsp (30 mL) Dijon mustard
1 tbsp (15 mL) Worcestershire sauce
¼ tsp (1 mL) salt
Juice of 1 lemon
1⅓ cups (325 mL) canola oil

In a medium bowl, whisk together red wine vinegar, balsamic vinegar, honey, mustard, Worcestershire sauce, salt, and lemon juice until well combined. Slowly whisk in oil until emulsified.

Transfer vinaigrette to a container, cover, and refrigerate until ready to use.

Yogurt Dill Jalapeño Dressing

Makes about 1 cup (250 mL)

½ cup (125 mL) chopped dill
½ cup (125 mL) yogurt
Juice of ½ lemon
1 tbsp (15 mL) honey
1 tsp (5 mL) minced jalapeño pepper
Salt and pepper

In a small bowl, whisk together dill, yogurt, lemon juice, honey, and jalapeño. Season to taste with salt and pepper.

Transfer dressing to a container, cover, and refrigerate until ready to use.

Buttermilk Basil Ranch Dressing

Makes about 1½ cups (375 mL)

1 cup (250 mL) buttermilk
¼ cup (60 mL) mayonnaise
¼ cup (60 mL) sour cream
1 tbsp (15 mL) white wine vinegar
3 tbsp (45 mL) finely chopped basil
2 tbsp (30 mL) finely chopped chives
1 clove garlic, minced
Salt and pepper

In a medium bowl, whisk together buttermilk, mayonnaise, sour cream, and vinegar until well combined, then stir in basil, chives, and garlic. Season to taste with salt and pepper. Transfer dressing to a container, cover, and refrigerate; use within 3 days.

Honey Mustard Vinaigrette

Makes 1¼ cups (300 mL)

2 tbsp (30 mL) Dijon mustard
2 tbsp (30 mL) honey
¼ cup (60 mL) white wine vinegar
½ cup (125 mL) vegetable or canola oil
¼ cup (60 mL) extra-virgin olive oil
Salt and pepper

In a small bowl, whisk together mustard, honey, and vinegar until well combined. Slowly whisk in vegetable oil and olive oil until emulsified. Season to taste with salt and pepper.

Transfer vinaigrette to a container, cover, and refrigerate until ready to use.

Green Goddess Dressing with Shallot & Herbs

Makes 1½ cups (375 mL)

....

1 ripe avocado, peeled
1 shallot, chopped
1 clove garlic, peeled
1 cup (250 mL) mayonnaise
½ cup (125 mL) sour cream
½ cup (125 mL) loosely packed flat-leaf parsley leaves
2 tbsp (30 mL) chopped chives
2 tbsp (30 mL) lemon juice
Salt and pepper

....

Place avocado, shallot, garlic, mayonnaise, sour cream, parsley, chives, and lemon juice in a blender and process until smooth. Season to taste with salt and pepper.

Transfer dressing to a container, cover, and refrigerate until ready to use.

Pistachio Lemon Vinaigrette

Makes 1¼ cups (300 mL)

....

¼ cup (60 mL) lemon juice
1 tbsp (15 mL) Dijon mustard
1 tsp (5 mL) granulated sugar
1 shallot, minced
½ cup (125 mL) vegetable or canola oil
¼ cup (60 mL) extra-virgin olive oil
¼ cup (60 mL) finely chopped pistachios
Salt and pepper

....

Whisk together lemon juice, mustard, sugar, and shallot until well combined. Slowly whisk in vegetable oil and olive oil until emulsified. Stir in pistachios and season to taste with salt and pepper.

Transfer vinaigrette to a container, cover, and refrigerate until ready to use.

Roasted Garlic & Anchovy Vinaigrette

Makes about 2½ cups (625 mL)

....

3 egg yolks
2 tbsp (30 mL) red wine vinegar
1 tbsp (15 mL) Dijon mustard
2 cups (500 mL) canola or vegetable oil
3 tbsp (45 mL) lemon juice
4 cloves roasted garlic, mashed to a paste
3 anchovies, chopped
3 tbsp (45 mL) grated Parmesan cheese
Salt and pepper

....

In a large bowl, whisk together egg yolks, vinegar, and mustard until well combined. Slowly whisk in oil until emulsified.

Whisk in lemon juice and garlic until thickened to desired consistency. Whisk in anchovies and Parmesan. Season to taste with salt and pepper.

Transfer vinaigrette to a container, cover, and refrigerate until ready to use.

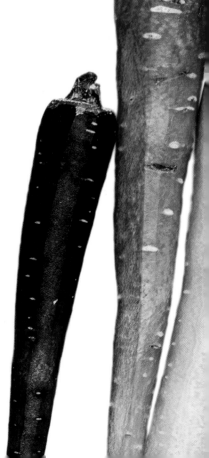

SALAD TOPPERS

Salad toppings can make a salad even more special and delicious. These toppings are all quick fixes to make your salad an **exciting start** to a great meal.

Candied Black Olives

Crispy Prosciutto Crackling

Blistered Balsamic & Basil Kissed Tomatoes

Brown Butter
Croutons

Espelette-Spiced
Pistachios

Brown Butter Croutons

Makes about 2 cups (500 mL)

....

½ loaf good-quality baguette, cut in 1-inch (2.5 cm) cubes
   (2 cups/500 mL)
4 tbsp (60 mL) butter
1 tbsp (15 mL) chopped flat-leaf parsley

....

Preheat oven to 375°F (190°C).

Place bread cubes in a medium bowl.

In a small saucepan over medium heat, melt butter and allow to brown slightly. Pour over bread cubes and toss until evenly coated.

Spread bread cubes in a single layer on a parchment-lined baking sheet. Bake, stirring a few times, until crisp and golden, about 10 minutes. Toss with chopped parsley.

Goat Cheese Thyme Frico

Makes 1 frico

....

1 log (5 oz/140 g) firm goat cheese
Leaves from 2 sprigs thyme
¼ tsp (1 mL) cracked black pepper

....

Preheat oven to 375°F (190°C).

Crumble goat cheese onto a parchment-lined baking sheet, forming a circle about ¼ inch (5 mm) thick. Sprinkle with thyme and pepper.

Bake until golden brown, about 15 minutes. Let frico cool completely before crumbling onto salad.

Espelette-Spiced Pistachios

Makes about 1 cup (250 mL)

....

1 tbsp (15 mL) olive oil
¼ tsp (1 mL) ground Espelette pepper
1 cup (250 mL) shelled raw pistachios
2 tbsp (30 mL) honey
¼ tsp (1 mL) salt

....

In a small saucepan, combine olive oil and Espelette pepper. Stir over medium heat until pepper darkens slightly, then stir in pistachios, honey, and salt. Cook, stirring frequently, until nuts are glossy, about 5 minutes.

Spread pistachios in a single layer on a plate and let cool completely before using.

Blistered Balsamic & Basil Kissed Tomatoes

Makes about 2 cups (500 mL)

....

1 pint (500 mL) cherry tomatoes
2 tbsp (30 mL) olive oil
2 tbsp (30 mL) balsamic vinegar
Leaves from 1 large sprig basil
Salt and pepper

....

Preheat oven to 375°F (190°C).

Place tomatoes on a baking sheet and toss with oil to coat. Roast until blistered, about 10 minutes.

Transfer tomatoes to a bowl and toss with vinegar and basil. Season to taste with salt and pepper. Let tomatoes rest at room temperature to allow flavors to infuse, about 15 minutes, before serving.

Crispy Prosciutto Crackling

Makes 6 pieces

6 thin slices prosciutto

Preheat oven to 375°F (190°C).

Place prosciutto slices in a single layer on a parchment-lined baking sheet. Cover with a second piece of parchment and a second baking sheet.

Bake prosciutto until evenly browned and crisp, about 15 minutes. Use the slices whole or break them up.

Quick Pickles

Makes 1 cup (250 mL)

．．．．．．．．．

1 cup (250 mL) vegetables sliced ¼ inch (5 mm) thick
  or cut in thin wedges (radishes, baby cucumbers,
  baby beets, etc.)
1 tbsp (15 mL) granulated sugar
¼ tsp (1 mL) salt

．．．．．．．．．

Place vegetables in a small bowl; add sugar and
salt and stir to combine. Let stand for 10 minutes
before using.

Crispy Onion Rings

Makes about 2 cups (500 mL)

．．．．．．．．．

1 white onion
¼ cup (60 mL) cornstarch
½ tsp (2 mL) salt
1½ cups (375 mL) vegetable oil

．．．．．．．．．

Using a mandoline, slice onion into ¹⁄₁₆-inch (1 mm)
slices. Separate rings. Toss rings with cornstarch
and salt until well coated.

In a medium, deep saucepan over medium heat,
heat oil to 350°F (180°C). Working in small batches,
add onions to oil and fry, stirring frequently, until
crisp and golden, about 10 minutes. Transfer to
paper towels to drain. Serve immediately.

Chili Orange Fried Chickpeas

Makes 1 cup (250 mL)

．．．．．．．．．

1 cup (250 mL) vegetable oil
1 cup (250 mL) canned chickpeas, drained,
  rinsed, and patted dry
1 tsp (5 mL) grated orange zest
¼ tsp (1 mL) cayenne pepper
¼ tsp (1 mL) salt

．．．．．．．．．

In a small, deep saucepan over medium heat, heat
oil to 350°F (180°C).

Working in batches if necessary, carefully add
chickpeas to hot oil and fry, stirring frequently, until
crispy, about 10 minutes.

With a slotted spoon, transfer chickpeas to a bowl
and toss with orange zest, cayenne, and salt. Let rest
for 5 minutes before serving.

Crispy Onion Rings

Candied Black Olives

Makes 1 cup (250 mL)

....

1 cup (250 mL) pitted black olives, patted dry
2 tbsp (30 mL) maple syrup

....

Preheat oven to 250°F.

Stir olives and syrup together until well combined, then spread in a single layer on a parchment-lined baking sheet. Bake until olives are dry, about 3 hours. Turn off oven and let cool for about 1 hour.

Pickled Jalapeño Peppers

Makes 1 cup (250 mL)

....

1 cup (250 mL) thinly sliced jalapeño peppers
¼ cup (60 mL) granulated sugar
¼ cup (60 mL) white wine
¼ cup (60 mL) white wine vinegar
¼ cup (60 mL) water
1 tsp (5 mL) salt

....

Place jalapeños in a small bowl.

In a medium saucepan, combine sugar, wine, vinegar, water, and salt. Bring to a boil over medium heat and cook, stirring occasionally, until sugar has dissolved, about 2 minutes. Pour hot pickling liquid over jalapeños, cover, and refrigerate for at least 24 hours before using.

Shaved Fennel

Makes about 4 cups (1 L)

....

1 fennel bulb, stalks discarded
Juice of ½ lemon
1 tbsp (15 mL) extra-virgin olive oil
Salt and pepper

....

Using a mandoline, very thinly shave fennel crosswise. Toss together fennel, lemon juice, and oil. Season to taste with salt and pepper. Let mixture sit at room temperature for 5 minutes, then cover and refrigerate for up to 2 hours.

Chili Orange Fried Chickpeas

Everything Green Salad with Green Goddess Dressing

·········

I love salads to be filled with lots of vegetables rather than lots of lettuce. I add Boston lettuce to this one for its buttery flavor and wonderful silkiness, but otherwise I stick to beautiful robust green vegetables. The peas and asparagus—bright green, warm, and sweet— will stand out, complemented by the avocado's creaminess, the dill's freshness, and the feta's saltiness. *Serves 4*

·········

½ cup (125 mL) sugar snap peas

4 spears asparagus, trimmed and cut in 2-inch (5 cm) pieces

1 baby cucumber, sliced

1 small zucchini, cut in ribbons with a vegetable peeler

1 head Boston lettuce, torn into bite-size pieces

2 green onions, sliced

1 small avocado, peeled and cut in wedges

2 sprigs dill, coarsely chopped

2 oz (55 g) feta cheese, crumbled

½ cup (125 mL) Green Goddess Dressing (page 61)

Salt and pepper

·········

Half fill a medium saucepan with cold salted water and bring to a boil over medium-high heat.

Add snap peas and boil for 1 minute. Using a slotted spoon, transfer to a bowl of ice water to stop cooking process and set color. Boil asparagus for 1 minute, then transfer to ice water. When cooled, drain peas and asparagus on paper towels.

In a large bowl, gently toss together peas, asparagus, cucumber, zucchini, lettuce, green onions, avocado, dill, and feta. Add dressing and toss until salad is well coated. Season to taste with salt and pepper and serve immediately.

Quinoa Salad with Roasted Squash, Cashews & Gouda

·········

My team at the restaurant will laugh when they see this one! I always pull long faces when quinoa is mentioned, an unconscious reaction that probably dates back to some less than great meal in the '90s. But actually I like quinoa. I like it even more combined with cashews and spice-roasted butternut squash, crisp apples, pickled beets, and beautifully aged Thunder Oak Gouda. The flavors and textures are rich and varied. This dish is colorful, warm, and just plain delicious. *Serves 4*

·········

1 cup (250 mL) diced butternut squash

⅓ cup (75 mL) whole cashews

½ tsp (2 mL) red pepper flakes

1 red apple, cut in wedges

2 green onions, thinly sliced

½ cup (125 mL) Brown Derby Vinaigrette (page 60)

Salt and pepper

4 cups (1 L) cooked red quinoa, cooled

½ cup (125 mL) pickled beets, cut in wedges

½ cup (125 mL) shaved Thunder Oak Gouda cheese

·········

Preheat oven to 375°F (190°C).

On a parchment-lined baking sheet, toss squash with cashews and red pepper flakes. Spread in a single layer. Roast until squash is golden brown and fork-tender, about 15 minutes.

In a large bowl, gently toss together squash, cashews, apple, and green onions. Add dressing and toss until salad is well coated. Season to taste with salt and pepper.

Mound quinoa onto a platter, spoon over squash mixture, and top with beets and cheese. Serve immediately.

Bloody Mary Shrimp Salad

I am obsessed with this salad. It combines two of my all-time favorites, shrimp and a Bloody Mary. I leave out the vodka, but otherwise the cocktail recipe is kept intact. Use fresh large shrimp. *Serves 4*

....

Grated zest and juice of 1 lemon

¼ cup (60 mL) vegetable oil

1 tsp (5 mL) prepared horseradish

1 tsp (5 mL) Worcestershire sauce

1 tsp (5 mL) hot sauce

½ tsp (2 mL) celery salt

16 shrimp (size 21/25), peeled, deveined, and cooked

1 pint (500 mL) cherry tomatoes, halved

1 cup (250 mL) celery leaves

1 handful basil leaves

½ cup (125 mL) mayonnaise

1 tbsp (15 mL) grated fresh horseradish

Salt and pepper

....

In a large bowl, stir together half of the lemon zest and juice, the vegetable oil, prepared horseradish, Worcestershire sauce, hot sauce, and celery salt. Add shrimp and toss gently. Let sit for 10 minutes.

Add cherry tomatoes, celery leaves, and basil.

In another bowl, whisk together mayonnaise, grated horseradish, and remaining lemon zest and juice. Season to taste with salt and pepper.

Spoon shrimp mixture onto a platter and serve with horseradish mayonnaise on the side.

This salad is perfect for summer evenings. It's sweet and salty, tangy and meaty.

Iceberg Salad with Blue Cheese & Bacon

To this classic salad, I've added my Buttermilk Basil Ranch Dressing, which is rich and balances the sharpness of the blue cheese and the sweetness of the tomatoes. For something extra-special, use smoked blue cheese. *Serves 4*

½ cup (125 mL) Buttermilk Basil Ranch Dressing (page 60)
1 iceberg lettuce, cut in quarters
½ cup (125 mL) crumbled blue cheese
1 cup (250 mL) cherry tomatoes, halved
2 green onions, thinly sliced
2 hard-boiled eggs, grated
4 slices cooked crispy bacon, crumbled

Spoon 1 tbsp (15 mL) dressing on each of 4 plates. Place a wedge of lettuce on top.

Divide cheese, tomatoes, green onions, eggs, and bacon over each salad and drizzle with remaining dressing. Serve immediately.

Salt-Baked Pear Salad with Goat Cheese & Pistachios

When pears are in season, I often feature variations on this salad at the restaurant. It's impressive and different and it tastes fantastic. There's a lot going on in this recipe, and you'll need to prepare the pears well in advance, but the result is memorable. The pears become so tender from the salt-baking. Their sweetness is balanced with the endive's pepperiness and the dried cranberries' tartness. The pistachio dressing is crunchy and acidic, combining perfectly with the lemon thyme honey. I keep these two on hand at all times. *Serves 4*

5 cups (1.25 L) kosher salt

4 star anise

2 cinnamon sticks, broken in pieces

1 tbsp (15 mL) pink peppercorns

6 Bosc pears

½ cup (125 mL) crumbled firm goat cheese

⅓ cup (75 mL) sour cream

Salt and pepper

1 bunch watercress, thick stems removed

2 Belgian endives, each cut in 8 wedges

⅓ cup (75 mL) sun-dried cranberries

⅓ cup (75 mL) Pistachio Lemon Vinaigrette
 (page 61)

Chopped pistachios, for garnish

¼ cup (60 mL) Lemon Thyme Honey (page 13)

Preheat oven to 375°F (190°C).

In a large bowl, stir together salt, star anise, cinnamon sticks, and peppercorns.

In a deep ovenproof cooking vessel, stand pears upright. Bury all but the tip and stem with the salt mixture. Bake until pears are fork-tender, about 45 minutes.

Let pears cool completely in salt mixture, then remove and brush off any salt that may be stuck to them. Discard salt mixture. Halve 2 pears lengthwise, core, and cut each into 8 wedges. Reserve remaining pears for another use.

In a small bowl, whisk together goat cheese and sour cream until smooth. Season to taste with salt and pepper. Spread a large spoonful across each of 4 plates.

Combine watercress, endives, cranberries, and pear wedges, then gently toss with vinaigrette. Mound on top of goat cheese mixture. Garnish each salad with chopped pistachios and a drizzle of honey. Serve immediately.

Note: You will have 4 pears left over. They are great served on a cheese tray with goat cheese or Brie.

Chopped Salad with Crispy Salami

This salad has everything, from charcuterie to three different greens, legumes to sun-dried tomatoes, and Parmesan to olives. Still, once the grocery shopping has been done, this salad is easily prepared. For something different, switch out the salami for Crispy Prosciutto Crackling (page 65). *Serves 4*

¼ cup (60 mL) thinly sliced salami cut in thin strips

1 head romaine lettuce, chopped in ¼-inch (5 mm) pieces

1 head radicchio, chopped in ¼-inch (5 mm) pieces

1 endive, chopped in ¼-inch (5 mm) pieces

⅓ cup (75 mL) finely chopped sun-dried tomatoes

1 cup (250 mL) canned chickpeas, drained and rinsed

½ cup (125 mL) pitted oil-cured olives, chopped

¼ cup (60 mL) sliced peperoncini

⅓ cup (75 mL) Brown Derby Vinaigrette (page 60)

⅓ cup (75 mL) grated Parmesan cheese

Salt and pepper

In a small nonstick skillet over medium heat, cook salami until crisp. Set aside.

In a large bowl, combine romaine, radicchio, endive, sun-dried tomatoes, chickpeas, olives, and peperoncini. Pour over dressing and toss to coat.

Divide salad among 4 plates. Top with crumbled salami and a sprinkling of Parmesan. Season to taste with salt and pepper and serve immediately.

Indian Spiced Lentil Salad

This salad is about ease. It tastes delicious and is simple to prepare. I use canned lentils for speed, but if you have time, don't hesitate to cook the lentils from scratch. The same goes for the pappadam, an Indian and Sri Lankan flatbread. It's not difficult to make, but if you can find it for purchase somewhere in your neighborhood, you'll get to eat that much sooner. Work fast and enjoy! *Serves 4*

4 pappadams
1 can (19 oz/540 mL) green lentils, drained and rinsed
2 heirloom carrots, shaved into ribbons with a vegetable peeler
1 cup (250 mL) cilantro leaves
½ cup (125 mL) seedless raisins
½ cup (125 mL) sliced almonds
⅓ cup (75 mL) Honey Mustard Vinaigrette (page 60)
Salt and pepper

Cook pappadams according to package directions. Set aside.

In a large bowl, combine lentils, carrots, cilantro, raisins, and almonds. Pour over dressing and toss gently to coat. Season to taste with salt and pepper.

Divide salad among 4 plates and serve with pappadams.

Chef Lora's Potato Salad

You all know the extremely talented Chef Lora Kirk! Lora makes, hands down, the best potato salad I've ever eaten. The key ingredient, after the potatoes, is the homemade pickled jalapeños, which add an amazing heat and piquant finish ... oh, and the caramelized onions, so good ... and the fresh dill ... Like I said, the best potato salad I've ever had! *Serves 4*

·········

2 lb (900 g) tri-colored mini potatoes, halved

1 tbsp (15 mL) olive oil

1 tbsp (15 mL) butter

2 small white onions, thinly sliced

2 tbsp (30 mL) thyme leaves

⅓ cup (75 mL) chopped dill

⅓ cup (75 mL) mayonnaise

2 dill pickles, thinly sliced

1 tbsp (15 mL) finely chopped Pickled Jalapeño Peppers (page 67)

1 tbsp (15 mL) pickled jalapeño liquid, or to taste

4 tsp (20 mL) salt

Cracked black pepper

·········

Place potatoes in a large pot of cold salted water, bring to a boil over medium-high heat, then reduce heat to low and simmer until potatoes are fork-tender, about 15 minutes. Drain and let cool for 10 minutes.

Meanwhile, in a medium skillet over medium-low heat, heat oil and melt butter. Add onions and thyme and cook, stirring occasionally, until onions are golden brown, about 15 minutes. Transfer onions to a plate and let cool slightly.

In a large bowl, stir together dill, mayonnaise, pickles, pickled jalapeños, pickled jalapeño liquid, and salt. Gently fold in potatoes and onions. Season to taste with black pepper and serve immediately.

IN THE OVEN

Creamy Mushroom & Spinach Lasagna

Lasagna is everyone's childhood favorite. It always seemed so much more special than all the other pastas. It's fun to make, too. This version is the perfect vegetarian dish. The mushrooms add an earthiness, and the spinach is smooth and substantial. The star, though, is the creamy delicious buffalo mozzarella. Don't leave it out!

Serves 6 to 8

Béchamel Sauce

½ cup (125 mL) butter

4 shallots, finely chopped

½ cup (125 mL) all-purpose flour

4 cups (1 L) whole (3.25%) milk

2 cups (500 mL) grated Parmesan cheese

½ cup (125 mL) chopped basil

1 tsp (5 mL) freshly grated nutmeg

Filling

1 tbsp (15 mL) olive oil

1 tbsp (15 mL) unsalted butter

2 lb (900 g) white mushrooms, sliced

4 cups (1 L) chopped baby spinach

4 cloves garlic, minced

Salt and pepper

1 lb (450 g) oven-ready lasagna noodles

8 oz (225 g) buffalo mozzarella, thinly sliced

2 cups (500 mL) shredded mozzarella cheese

continued . . .

Preheat oven to 375°F (190°C).

For the béchamel sauce, in a medium saucepan over medium heat, melt butter. Add shallots and cook, stirring frequently, for 3 minutes. Add flour and cook, stirring, for 2 minutes. Whisk in milk. Bring to a boil, then reduce heat to medium-low and simmer, stirring frequently, until sauce is thick enough to coat the back of a spoon, about 5 minutes. Add Parmesan, basil, and nutmeg and whisk until smooth. Keep sauce warm.

For the filling, in a large skillet over medium-high heat, heat olive oil and melt butter. Add mushrooms and sauté until liquid has evaporated and mushrooms have started to caramelize, about 10 minutes.

Stir in spinach and garlic and cook until spinach has wilted and garlic has softened, about 5 minutes more. Season to taste with salt and pepper.

Spread one-third of the béchamel sauce in a buttered 13- × 9-inch (3 L) baking dish. Arrange 4 lasagna noodles on top. Spoon half of the mushroom-spinach mixture evenly over noodles, then layer with half of the buffalo mozzarella. Repeat layering one more time, ending with béchamel on top.

Sprinkle evenly with shredded mozzarella. Cover with a piece of buttered parchment paper followed by a piece of foil.

Bake for 1 hour. Remove foil and parchment, increase oven temperature to 500°F (260°C), and bake until top is golden, about 15 minutes more. Transfer lasagna to a rack and let cool for 20 minutes before serving.

Salt-Baked Fish with Aromatics

The salt-baking technique both looks fantastic and results in the most tender and moist fish. The salt pack hardens in the oven, allowing the fish to steam in its own juices with the herbs and citrus. To serve, present the salt-packed fish to the table and then wallop the shell like you would crème brûlée, cracking it to reveal the beautiful cooked fish inside. *Serves 4*

3 lb (1.35 kg) Diamond Crystal brand kosher salt

Grated zest of 2 large lemons

8 sprigs thyme, chopped

4 sprigs rosemary, chopped

1 tbsp (15 mL) red pepper flakes

5 large egg whites, beaten

1 cleaned whole fish of your choice (about 2 lb/900 g), rinsed and patted dry

Olive oil and lemon wedges, for garnish

Preheat oven to 400°F (200°C).

In a large bowl, stir together salt, lemon zest, thyme, rosemary, and red pepper flakes. Add egg whites and continue stirring until mixture resembles wet sand.

Place half of the salt mixture in the bottom of a baking dish that is slightly larger than the fish. Lay fish on top and cover completely with remaining salt mixture, packing it down, and leaving tail end exposed, if necessary.

Bake fish for 25 minutes or until cooked through.

To serve, gently crack salt layer with the back of a spoon to expose fish. Most of the skin will come off, too. Use a sharp knife to gently remove any skin that remains on the fish. Fillet fish into 4 portions and transfer to slightly warmed plates. Serve with a drizzle of olive oil and a lemon wedge.

Halibut with Chorizo, Clams & Fennel

Think of this dish as an at-home clambake. This recipe highlights the halibut, but the idea is the same: tossing together amazing ingredients and baking until the fish has cooked in the wonderful juices rendered from the sausage and vegetables. This dish is fun to make and even more fun to share. Perfect in the oven or even on the barbecue. *Serves 6*

1 large fennel bulb
1 lb (450 g) fingerling potatoes, halved lengthwise
4 tbsp (60 mL) olive oil
1 lb (450 g) cured chorizo sausage, cut in ¼-inch (5 mm) slices
1 onion, thickly sliced
6 skinless halibut fillets (4 oz/115 g each)
1 lemon, cut in ¼-inch (5 mm) slices
2 sprigs thyme
2 tsp (10 mL) thyme leaves
½ cup (125 mL) pitted mixed olives
12 littleneck clams
½ cup (125 mL) white wine

Preheat oven to 475°F (240°C). Discard stalks from fennel, then halve bulb lengthwise and cut into ¼-inch (5 mm) wedges.

Bring a large pot of water to a boil over medium-high heat. Add fennel and blanch until fork-tender, about 4 minutes. With a slotted spoon, transfer fennel to a dish and set aside.

Add potatoes to boiling water, reduce heat to medium, and simmer until tender, about 10 minutes. Drain potatoes and set aside.

In a large skillet over medium-high heat, combine 2 tbsp (30 mL) oil, chorizo, and onion; sauté until chorizo is browned, about 5 minutes.

On a baking sheet, place a piece of foil large enough to encase the fish and other ingredients.

Rub halibut with remaining 2 tbsp (30 mL) oil and place on foil. Arrange lemon slices, thyme sprigs, thyme leaves, fennel, potatoes, chorizo mixture, olives, and clams around halibut. Drizzle with wine. Fold foil over to cover fish and crimp edges to create a tightly sealed packet.

Bake for 35 minutes. Let packet rest for 5 minutes before opening. Be careful, the steam inside will be hot!

Bacon-Wrapped Trout with Pecan Stuffing

·········

Trout is salmon's often overlooked cousin. But despite its smaller size, this freshwater fish is packed with delicate and delicious meat. It doesn't take much to overpower trout's understated flavors, so I like to keep it simple. The bacon keeps the meat from drying out. Its fat renders, basting the fish and absorbing into the stuffing. The pecan stuffing adds an aromatic element that smells delicious and tastes phenomenal. *Serves 4*

·········

4 tbsp (60 mL) butter

2 shallots, chopped

2 celery stalks, diced

1 cup (250 mL) pecans, chopped

Leaves from 2 sprigs thyme

1 tbsp (15 mL) chopped parsley

3 slices brioche, torn in 1-inch (2.5 cm) pieces

½ cup (125 mL) heavy (35%) cream

2 cleaned whole trout (about 2 lb/900 g each), rinsed and patted dry

8 slices bacon

In a medium skillet over medium heat, melt butter. Add shallots and celery and sauté until tender-crisp, about 5 minutes. Remove pan from heat.

In a medium bowl, stir together pecans, thyme, parsley, brioche, and cream. Stir in shallot mixture. Let sit for 10 minutes.

Divide stuffing in half and stuff into cavity of each trout. Wrap 4 pieces of bacon around each trout and stand fish upright (belly down) on a baking sheet.

Bake for 25 minutes. Let rest for 5 minutes before serving.

Chicken & Asparagus à la King

When I was growing up, my parents loved throwing dinner parties. This recipe is one that I loved to make with my mom. Thinking back on those memories, I always smile … This retro dish is packed with deliciousness. It's warm and rich and nestled in crisp vol-au-vent pastries. Whatever the current foodie trends, I continue to love and promote the noble vol-au-vent. *Serves 4*

1 tbsp (15 mL) olive oil

2 tbsp (30 mL) butter

2 boneless, skinless chicken breasts, cut in 1-inch (2.5 cm) pieces

1 leek, white part only, finely chopped

2 shallots, finely chopped

1 cup (250 mL) asparagus cut on the diagonal in 1-inch (2.5 cm) pieces

1 sprig thyme

½ cup (125 mL) white wine

2 cups (500 mL) heavy (35%) cream

4 frozen vol-au-vent pastry cups, baked

In a medium skillet over medium-high heat, heat oil and melt butter. Add chicken and sauté until no pink remains, about 10 minutes. Add leek and sauté for 5 minutes. Add shallots, asparagus, and thyme; cook for 3 minutes more, stirring frequently.

Add wine and scrape up any brown bits stuck to the bottom of the skillet. Stir in cream and continue cooking until sauce has reduced by half. Remove thyme sprig.

Spoon chicken mixture into pastry cups and serve immediately.

Chicken with Lots of Cloves of Garlic

....

I would make this dish for the aroma alone. The caramelizing garlic cloves smell like heaven. This dish is another great recipe for dinner parties. It's easily prepared in advance, and the sweet scent from the oven will guarantee hungry guests, while the scrumptious results will guarantee happy guests. *Serves 6 to 8*

....

3 tbsp (45 mL) olive oil

1 chicken (about 4 lb/1.8 kg), backbone removed, cut in 8 pieces

Salt and pepper

1 cup (250 mL) peeled whole garlic cloves

½ cup (125 mL) white wine

1 cup (250 mL) chicken stock

1 tbsp (15 mL) chopped tarragon

....

Preheat oven to 350°F (180°C).

In a heavy pot over medium-high heat, heat oil. Season chicken with salt and pepper. Add chicken to pot and cook, turning once, until browned, about 8 minutes per side. Transfer chicken to a baking dish.

Add garlic to pot and sauté until browned, about 6 minutes. Add wine and scrape up any brown bits stuck to the bottom of the pot. Add stock and bring mixture to a boil. Using a slotted spoon, transfer one-quarter of the garlic to the baking dish with chicken. Mash remaining garlic into stock and pour over chicken.

Bake until chicken is tender and no pink remains inside, about 20 minutes. Garnish with tarragon just before serving.

Rib Roast with Horseradish Salt Crust

....

A perfect Sunday roast! *Serves 8*

....

2 large white onions, cut in 1-inch (2.5 cm) slices

¼ cup (60 mL) Dijon mustard

1 standing prime rib roast (about 6 lb/2.7 kg)

1½ cups (375 mL) kosher salt

⅓ cup (75 mL) prepared horseradish

2 tbsp (30 mL) mustard seeds

2 tbsp (30 mL) thyme leaves

2 tbsp (30 mL) rosemary leaves

2 tbsp (30 mL) cracked black pepper

5 bay leaves, crumbled

3 egg whites, whipped until frothy

Preheat oven to 450°F (230°C).

Layer onion slices in a roasting pan. Set aside.

Slather mustard evenly over prime rib. Set aside.

In a large bowl, combine salt, horseradish, mustard seeds, thyme, rosemary, pepper, and bay leaves. Add egg whites and stir until mixture resembles wet sand. Press salt mixture evenly onto fatty side and ends of prime rib, then place bone side down on onions in roasting pan.

Roast for 15 minutes. Reduce oven temperature to 325°F (160°C) and continue roasting for 20 minutes per pound (450 g) or until an instant-read thermometer inserted in thickest part of roast registers 130°F (55°C) for medium-rare doneness.

Transfer prime rib to a cutting board and let rest for 20 minutes. Remove and discard salt crust before slicing meat.

Porchetta

. . . .

I love the Italian cooking tradition for so many reasons, not least for bringing us porchetta. This moist boneless pork roast is brined and then stuffed with herbs and spices. These gorgeous layers are then rolled and roasted. It takes some time to prepare, but is absolutely worth the effort. *Serves 10 to 12*

. . . .

Dry Rub

2 tbsp (30 mL) thyme leaves

1½ tsp (7 mL) kosher salt

1 tsp (5 mL) each onion powder and garlic powder

1 tsp (5 mL) each dried oregano and dried basil

½ tsp (2 mL) dried thyme

½ tsp (2 mL) black pepper

½ tsp (2 mL) cayenne pepper

Brine and Porchetta

16 cups (3.8 L) cold water

8 sprigs thyme

8 sprigs rosemary

8 bay leaves

6 cloves garlic, smashed

¼ cup (60 mL) black peppercorns

2 tbsp (30 mL) fennel seeds

1 tbsp (15 mL) red pepper flakes

1¼ cups (300 mL) kosher salt

¼ cup (60 mL) brown sugar

2 tbsp (30 mL) honey

1 meaty skin-on pork belly (about 9 lb/4.1 kg)

¼ cup (60 mL) Dijon mustard

. . . .

For the dry rub, mix all ingredients thoroughly. Store in an airtight container until ready to use.

For the brine, in a large pot, combine water, thyme, rosemary, bay leaves, garlic, peppercorns, fennel seeds, and red pepper flakes. Bring to a boil, then reduce heat to medium-low. Add salt, sugar, and honey; cook until salt and sugar have dissolved.

Pour brine into a roasting pan and let cool to room temperature. Add pork belly, skin side up, cover, and refrigerate for at least 12 hours.

Remove pork belly from brine (discarding brine) and pat dry. Smear all over with mustard, then rub all over with dry rub. Cover and refrigerate for 12 hours.

Preheat oven to 400°F (200°C).

Pierce pork skin all over with the tip of a knife. Place pork belly skin side down and, starting from a long side, roll belly to form a tight cylinder. Tie tightly with kitchen twine at 2-inch (5 cm) intervals.

Place porchetta in a roasting pan and roast for 1 hour. Reduce oven temperature to 300°F (150°C) and continue roasting about 2½ hours more or until the skin is golden brown and crispy and an instant-read thermometer registers 185°F (85°C). Transfer porchetta to a cutting board and let rest for 20 minutes before slicing.

Pork Roast with Prosciutto, Apricots & Squash

....

Pork wrapped in more pork! What's wrong with that? This dish is not, however, as meat-centric as it sounds. The butternut squash, cipollini onions, dried fruit, and rosemary are the focus here, giving this roast an incredible flavor palette that is reminiscent of North African tagines. Make sure to let the roast rest—the meat will become beautifully moist. *Serves 4*

....

2 cups (500 mL) diced butternut squash

12 cipollini onions, peeled

½ cup (125 mL) dried apricots, chopped

½ cup (125 mL) raisins

1 sprig rosemary

2 tbsp (30 mL) butter, melted

1 bone-in pork loin roast (about 3 lb/1.35 kg)

Salt and pepper

2 tbsp (30 mL) olive oil

4 slices prosciutto

....

Preheat oven to 375°F (190°C).

In a large bowl, toss together squash, onions, apricots, raisins, rosemary, and butter until well combined. Spread mixture in a single layer in a roasting pan. Set aside.

Season pork roast well with salt and pepper. In a medium skillet over medium-high heat, heat oil. Add pork and sear on all sides. Transfer to a plate and let cool for 15 minutes.

Wrap prosciutto slices around pork, then place on top of fruits and vegetables in roasting pan. Roast for 1½ hours or until an instant-read thermometer registers 160°F (70°C). Transfer roast to a cutting board and let rest for 10 minutes before slicing.

Rack of Lamb with Cumin, Almond & Mint Crust

Lamb is a real treat. Its flavor is wonderful and complex. The rack is extra-special, since the meat on the bones is packed with so much flavor. The ingredients for the crust might seem extensive, but in fact it's easily prepared and, more importantly, results in the most delicious accompaniment to this delicate meat. This crust is spiced and herbaceous, and really ups the ante in this dish. *Serves 4*

Leaves from 1 bunch mint
1 cup (250 mL) almonds, toasted
1 cup (250 mL) panko bread crumbs
2 tbsp (30 mL) ground cumin
1 tbsp (15 mL) turmeric
1 tsp (5 mL) ground thyme
1 tsp (5 mL) grated fresh ginger
½ tsp (2 mL) cinnamon
½ tsp (2 mL) red pepper flakes
2 tbsp (30 mL) olive oil
2 lamb racks
Salt and pepper
2 tbsp (30 mL) Dijon mustard
2 tbsp (30 mL) honey

Preheat oven to 350°F (180°C).

In a food processor, combine mint, almonds, panko, cumin, turmeric, thyme, ginger, cinnamon, red pepper flakes, and oil; process into a paste.

Season lamb racks with salt and pepper. Stir together mustard and honey; rub over lamb, then smear on spice paste.

Place racks bone side down in a roasting pan and roast for 20 minutes for medium-rare doneness. Let racks rest for 5 minutes before carving.

IN A PAN

Salmon with Mushrooms & Sweet Corn

··········

This incredibly simple dish combines three exceptional ingredients. I love salmon for its robust and distinct flavor. The salmon's crisped skin is fantastic! To get it right, dry the fillet thoroughly, removing as much moisture as possible from the skin. Then, when the oil in the skillet is hot, add the fillet skin side down. When the skin has crisped and released from the skillet, flip and cook the other side. The crispy skin adds texture to the dish, laying the foundation for the tender salmon meat, beautiful smoky chanterelles, and succulent sweet corn. This is the perfect late-summer meal. *Serves 4*

2 tbsp (30 mL) olive oil

4 skin-on center-cut salmon fillets (about 8 oz/225 g each)

2 tbsp (30 mL) unsalted butter

1 lb (450 g) button mushrooms, quartered

1 shallot, minced

1 cup (250 mL) fresh sweet corn kernels

2 tbsp (30 mL) finely chopped flat-leaf parsley

Salt and pepper

Preheat oven to 325°F (160°C).

In a large skillet over medium-high heat, heat oil. Place salmon skin side down in pan and cook until skin is crispy, about 4 minutes. Carefully turn over and cook for 4 minutes more for medium-rare doneness. Transfer salmon to a serving dish and keep warm in the oven.

Melt butter in the skillet. Add mushrooms and sauté until most of the liquid has evaporated, about 5 minutes. Stir in shallot and corn; cook, stirring frequently, until heated through, about 5 minutes more.

Stir in parsley and season to taste with salt and pepper. Spoon mushroom mixture over salmon fillets and serve immediately.

Chicken Curry

....

Curry is exotic and delicious. I just love how the Indian spices infuse the rich, sweet coconut milk. I make the curry sauce separately for two reasons. First, it allows me to play around with the proportions, sometimes making it hotter and sometimes sweeter. Second, I refrigerate the remaining sauce to use in a different recipe. *Serves 4*

....

Curry Sauce

¼ cup (60 mL) vegetable oil

1 lb (450 g) onions (about 3 medium), chopped

1 clove garlic, chopped

3 tbsp (45 mL) curry powder

1 tbsp (15 mL) garam masala

1 tsp (5 mL) cumin seeds

1 tsp (5 mL) ground cardamom

1 tsp (5 mL) turmeric

½ cup (125 mL) coconut milk

2 cups (500 mL) tomato juice

2 cups (500 mL) chicken stock

Salt, black pepper, and cayenne pepper

Chicken Curry

2 tbsp (30 mL) vegetable oil

1 lb (450 g) boneless, skinless chicken thighs, cut in 1-inch (2.5 cm) cubes

½ cup (125 mL) diced mixed bell peppers

½ cup (125 mL) diced carrot

½ cup (125 mL) diced celery

....

For the curry sauce, in a large saucepan over medium heat, combine oil and onions and cook, stirring frequently, until light brown, about 15 minutes.

Add garlic, curry powder, garam masala, cumin, cardamom, and turmeric; cook, stirring frequently, for 5 minutes. Reduce heat to low. Stir in coconut milk until well combined, then add tomato juice and stock. Simmer, uncovered and stirring occasionally, until sauce has thickened, about 1 hour.

Season sauce to taste with salt, black pepper, and cayenne; let cool for 10 minutes. Purée until smooth. Reserve 4 cups (1 L) curry sauce; refrigerate or freeze remaining curry sauce for another use.

For the chicken curry, in large saucepan over medium-high heat, heat oil. Add chicken and sauté until browned on all sides, about 10 minutes.

Add peppers, carrot, and celery and sauté until vegetables are tender-crisp, about 5 minutes. Stir in reserved curry sauce and bring mixture to a boil, stirring constantly. Reduce heat to medium-low and cook sauce for another 10 minutes. Serve immediately spooned over hot basmati rice.

Pasta Carbonara

....

What makes an authentic pasta carbonara remains controversial, but for me it's all about the bacon, egg, and freshly cracked pepper. This dish is simple to throw together, with rich flavor and beautiful silkiness. Just don't scramble the eggs! And don't be shy with the pepper. It cuts the rich sauce and gives the dish its distinct character and addictive quality. *Serves 4*

....

4 oz (115 g) pancetta (or other unsmoked bacon), diced
¾ cup (175 mL) heavy (35%) cream
4 eggs
½ cup (125 mL) grated Parmesan cheese, plus more for garnish
1 tsp (5 mL) freshly cracked black pepper
12 oz (340 g) spaghetti
¼ cup (60 mL) finely chopped flat-leaf parsley

....

In a large, heavy saucepan over medium heat, cook pancetta until just starting to crisp, about 5 minutes. Add cream and reduce heat to lowest setting. Keep warm.

Meanwhile, whisk together eggs, Parmesan, and black pepper. Set aside.

Cook spaghetti according to package directions until al dente. Drain, reserving ½ cup (125 mL) pasta water. Add spaghetti to cream mixture.

Pour egg mixture over spaghetti and stir constantly until well combined, adding a little reserved pasta water if necessary to thin out sauce.

Serve pasta immediately, garnished with a sprinkling of Parmesan and parsley.

Fast Ginger Chili Pork
with Asian Greens

....

I use the tenderloin in this dish because it's tender and lean and cooks super-quick, making this an easy dinner. The grain in the tenderloin catches all the wonderful citrus and sauces. I like to cook the bok choy just until it's bright green and still pops in your mouth. This is a delicious dish if you are hungry and need a quick fix. *Serves 4*

....

2 tbsp (30 mL) vegetable oil

1 pork tenderloin (about 1 lb/450 g), cut in ¼-inch (5 mm) slices

8 cups (2 L) sliced baby bok choy

1 tbsp (15 mL) minced fresh ginger

2 cloves garlic, minced

¼ cup (60 mL) soy sauce

Grated zest of ½ orange

¾ cup (175 mL) freshly squeezed orange juice

2 tsp (10 mL) sesame oil

1 bunch green onions, sliced

2 tbsp (30 mL) toasted sesame seeds

1 Thai red chili, very thinly sliced

....

In a large sauté pan over medium-high heat, heat oil. Add pork and stir-fry until no pink remains, about 3 minutes.

Add bok choy and stir-fry until tender-crisp, about 5 minutes. Add ginger and garlic; stir-fry for 1 minute more.

Stir in soy sauce, orange zest, orange juice, and sesame oil. Cover and steam mixture for 2 minutes. Turn out onto a platter, garnish with green onions, sesame seeds, and sliced chili, and serve immediately.

Pork Chops with Artichokes, Sausage & Rapini

Pork chops are so handsome. They're usually the workhorse in the kitchen, served mid-week with potatoes or side salad. But I think they deserve some extra-special care. This recipe is win-win: the chops get tenderized and dressed in beautiful ingredients, and you get to eat them! This dish combines different textures and tastes. The sausage adds heat, the rapini spice, the artichokes and olives silk and salt, and the raisins absorb all these amazing juices while caramelizing into bite-size treats. This dish is pure rustic excellence. *Serves 4*

....

⅓ cup (75 mL) seedless raisins

2 hot Italian sausages, casings removed

4 bone-in pork rib chops (about 6 oz/170 g each)

½ bunch rapini, cut in 2-inch (5 cm) pieces

1 can (14 oz/398 mL) artichoke hearts, drained and quartered

¼ cup (60 mL) pitted green olives

1 tbsp (15 mL) sherry vinegar

....

Soak raisins in hot water until plumped. Drain well and pat dry. Set aside.

In a large sauté pan over medium-high heat, crumble in sausage meat and cook, stirring frequently, until well browned, about 15 minutes. With a slotted spoon, transfer sausage to a plate.

Add pork chops to fat in pan and fry, turning once, for 4 minutes per side for medium doneness. Transfer chops to a plate and tent loosely with foil to keep warm.

Add rapini to pan and sauté until tender-crisp, about 3 minutes. Toss in raisins, artichokes, olives, and reserved sausage; cook until heated through, about 2 minutes more.

Deglaze pan with vinegar, scraping up any brown bits stuck to bottom of pan, then spoon mixture over pork chops. Serve immediately.

Sirloin Steaks with Oysters Rockefeller Butter

....

Everyone knows that I love oysters. But steak and oysters? You bet! This is a great surf-and-turf recipe. Use the freshest possible oysters, and I promise, you'll taste the difference. Packed with flavor, this butter will fire up your steak dinner to a whole new level. *Serves 2*

....

5 tbsp (75 mL) cold unsalted butter, cut in cubes

1 shallot, finely chopped

1 celery stalk, finely diced

¼ cup (60 mL) finely chopped fennel

1 clove garlic, minced

2 tbsp (30 mL) Pernod or other anise liqueur

1 bunch green onions, thinly sliced

Leaves from 2 sprigs thyme

½ cup (125 mL) parsley leaves

½ tsp (2 mL) hot sauce

2 boneless sirloin steaks (each 1 inch/2.5 cm thick and about 8 oz/225 g)

Salt and pepper

2 tbsp (30 mL) olive oil

6 shucked oysters, liquor reserved

....

In a small skillet over medium heat, melt 1 tbsp (15 mL) butter. Add shallot, celery, fennel, and garlic; cook, stirring frequently, until softened, about 5 minutes. Sir in Pernod and cook until evaporated, about 1 minute more.

Transfer mixture to a food processor and let cool slightly. Add green onions, thyme, parsley, hot sauce, and remaining 4 tbsp (60 mL) butter; process until smooth. Transfer mixture to a small bowl, cover, and refrigerate until needed.

Season steaks with salt and pepper. In a large, heavy skillet over medium-high heat, heat oil. Add steaks and cook, turning once, to medium-rare doneness, about 4 minutes per side. Transfer steaks to a serving plate, loosely tent with foil, and set aside.

To skillet, add oysters and oyster liquor and cook, stirring frequently, for 2 minutes. Turn off heat, spoon in reserved butter mixture, and cook, stirring constantly, until sauce has emulsified. Spoon oyster-butter sauce over steaks and serve immediately.

Adobo-Rubbed Rib-Eye Steak with Green Chili Aïoli

....

My favorite cut—the rib-eye! A great rib-eye steak must be thick, marbled, and medium-rare. If the steak is too thin, it won't develop the all-important caramelized crust, which will crisp this adobo rub. For the rub, make sure to toast the spices to bring out all their magic.

Serves 4

....

Adobo Rub and Steak

2 tbsp (30 mL) whole allspice

2 tbsp (30 mL) black peppercorns

1 tbsp (15 mL) cumin seeds

1 piece cinnamon stick (about 1½ inches/
   4 cm long), broken

7 whole cloves

2 tbsp (30 mL) sweet paprika

1 tbsp (15 mL) chipotle powder

1 tbsp (15 mL) ancho chili powder

¼ cup (60 mL) kosher salt

¼ cup (60 mL) granulated sugar

1 bone-in rib-eye steak (1½ inches/4 cm thick
   and about 1¼ lb/565 g)

Green Chili Aïoli

4 large cloves garlic, roasted and peeled

1 large poblano pepper, roasted, peeled, seeded,
   and coarsely chopped

1 jalapeño pepper, seeded and chopped

1 cup (250 mL) cilantro leaves

3 tbsp (45 mL) lime juice

½ tsp (2 mL) cumin seeds

1 large egg yolk

½ cup (125 mL) vegetable oil, plus more for grilling

....

For the adobo rub, in a small skillet over medium-high heat, dry-toast allspice, peppercorns, cumin seeds, cinnamon stick, and cloves, stirring constantly, until fragrant, about 1 minute. Let cool, then transfer to a spice grinder (or use a mortar and pestle). Add paprika, chipotle powder, ancho powder, salt, and sugar; process into a powder.

Sprinkle 1 tbsp (15 mL) adobo rub over each side of steak and let stand at room temperature for 30 minutes.

Meanwhile, for the aïoli, in a blender, combine roasted garlic, poblano, jalapeño, cilantro, lime juice, cumin seeds, and egg yolk; purée until smooth. With motor running, add oil a few drops at a time through feed tube until mixture is emulsified. Set aside.

Coat grill rack with vegetable oil and preheat barbecue to medium-high. Add steak and grill, turning once, for 6 minutes per side for medium-rare doneness. Let steak rest for 5 minutes before cutting against the grain into ½-inch (1 cm) slices. Serve immediately with aïoli.

Sweetbreads with Capers, Lemon & Brown Butter

....

Sweetbreads are one of the most prized offal cuts. I don't generally get excited about offal, but I go crazy for sweetbreads. They're tender and creamy and just plain delicious. But, because their preparation is more elaborate than with most dishes, sweetbreads are not popular with home cooks. I think it's time to change that, even for just one special occasion. This dish lets the sweetbreads shine, adding the brown butter for sweetness and the lemon and capers for citrus and salt. The combination is divine. *Serves 4*

....

1 lb (450 g) sweetbreads
Salt and pepper
2 tbsp (30 mL) olive oil
2 tbsp (30 mL) butter
1 shallot, finely chopped
2 cloves garlic, minced
Juice of ½ lemon
2 tbsp (30 mL) capers, rinsed
Leaves from 2 sprigs thyme
¼ cup (60 mL) chopped parsley

....

Wash sweetbreads under cold running water. Pat dry and season well with salt and pepper.

In a large skillet over medium-high heat, heat oil. Add sweetbreads and sauté until golden, about 6 minutes. Transfer sweetbreads to a bowl and set aside.

Add butter to skillet and cook until browned, about 2 minutes. Add shallot and garlic and sauté for 2 minutes more. Add lemon juice, capers, and thyme; cook for 1 minute, stirring frequently.

Return sweetbreads to skillet, stir in parsley, and season to taste with salt and pepper. Serve immediately.

Veal Chops with Bacon & Rosemary Cream

This dish is delicious and easy to prepare. The wonderful bacon flavor adds to the elegant taste of the veal. When the aromatic quality of the rosemary mingles with the cream, your mouth instantly starts to water. Pour yourself a nice glass of wine and enjoy this beautiful bistro-style classic. It works well with pork chops as well. *Serves 4*

4 slices bacon, diced
4 veal chops (about 6 oz/170 g each)
2 shallots, thinly sliced
1 clove garlic, minced
¼ cup (60 mL) white wine
Leaves from 1 sprig rosemary
½ cup (125 mL) heavy (35%) cream
Salt and pepper

Preheat oven to 200°F (100°C).

In a large skillet over medium heat, cook bacon, stirring frequently, until fat has rendered and bacon is crispy, about 5 minutes. With a slotted spoon, transfer bacon to paper towels to drain.

Add veal chops to skillet and cook, turning once, to medium-rare doneness, about 4 minutes per side. Transfer to a platter and keep warm in the oven.

Add shallots and garlic to skillet and cook, stirring, until soft, about 2 minutes. Stir in wine and cook until reduced by half.

Stir in rosemary, cream, and reserved bacon and cook until sauce is heated through, about 2 minutes. Season to taste with salt and pepper. Spoon over chops and serve immediately.

Duck à l'Orange

The French classic canard à l'orange features a whole roasted duck served with orange sauce. Duck à l'orange is in fact the British interpretation, made popular in the 1960s and then imported to North America to much fanfare, and for good reason too. Duck is delicious. It is packed with flavorful fats that make the meat extra-tender and luxurious. I love the classic, but in this recipe I make the sauce even more inviting by combining the orange with soy sauce, sweet spices, thyme, and honey. Oh, and hang on to your duck fat. Fried potatoes love duck fat. *Serves 4*

4 duck breasts (about 4 oz/115 g each)
Salt and pepper
2 navel oranges, peeled and segmented
½ cup (125 mL) soy sauce
2 tbsp (30 mL) honey
½ tsp (2 mL) cinnamon
1 cinnamon stick
3 star anise
2 tbsp (30 mL) butter
Leaves from 1 sprig thyme
Cracked black pepper

Preheat oven to 350°F (180°C).

Without cutting into the breast meat, make ¾-inch (2 cm) long diagonal incisions into the skin to create a diamond pattern. Season both sides of duck with salt and pepper.

In a large ovenproof skillet over medium-high heat, add duck breasts skin side down and cook until skin is golden brown and fat has rendered, about 7 minutes.

Turn breasts over and cook for 2 minutes more. Transfer skillet to oven and cook duck until an instant-read thermometer inserted in thickest part of breast registers 160°F (70°C) for medium-rare doneness, about 5 minutes. Transfer breasts to a plate and tent loosely with foil. Set aside.

Meanwhile, in a small skillet, combine orange segments, soy sauce, honey, cinnamon, cinnamon stick, and star anise. Cook over medium heat until reduced by half. Turn off heat and discard cinnamon stick and star anise. Whisk in butter and thyme. Season to taste with pepper.

Cut duck breasts crosswise into ¼-inch (5 mm) slices and fan on a platter. Spoon over sauce and serve immediately.

IN A POT

STOCKS

Chicken Stock

Makes about 3 quarts (3 L)

....

4 lb (1.8 kg) chicken bones (wings, backs, necks)

4 carrots, quartered

3 onions, quartered

4 celery stalks, quartered

1 leek, white and pale green parts only, cut in thirds

4 cloves garlic

6 sprigs parsley

3 sprigs thyme

2 bay leaves

¼ tsp (1 mL) black peppercorns

2 tsp (10 mL) salt

....

In a stockpot, combine chicken bones, carrots, onions, celery, leek, garlic, parsley, thyme, bay leaves, peppercorns, and salt. Add just enough cold water to cover bones. Bring to a boil, then reduce heat to low and simmer, uncovered, for 4 hours, skimming impurities from surface of stock as it cooks down.

Strain stock through a fine-mesh sieve into a container, discarding solids. Set container of stock in kitchen sink and surround with ice water to cool as quickly as possible. Store stock in refrigerator and use within a week, or freeze for up to 3 months.

Vegetable Stock

Makes about 2 quarts (2 L)

....

2 leeks, white part only, thinly sliced

6 carrots, cut in 1-inch (2.5 cm) rounds

3 celery stalks, thinly sliced

3 onions, thinly sliced

Stems from ¼ bunch tarragon

Stems from ¼ bunch basil

Stems from ¼ bunch chervil

1 star anise

5 white peppercorns

5 fennel seeds

1 cup (250 mL) white wine

½ lemon, sliced

....

Place leeks, carrots, celery, and onions in a stockpot and add just enough water to cover. Bring to a boil, then reduce heat to low and simmer for 10 minutes. Add herb stems, star anise, peppercorns, and fennel seeds; simmer for another 5 minutes. Remove pot from heat and stir in white wine and lemon slices.

Strain stock through a fine-mesh sieve into a container, discarding solids. Set container of stock in kitchen sink and surround with ice water to cool as quickly as possible. Store cooled stock in refrigerator and use within a week, or freeze for up to 3 months.

Fish Stock
Makes 2 quarts (2 L)

....

2 tbsp (30 mL) unsalted butter

1 celery stalk, cut in 1-inch pieces

1 onion, quartered

1 leek, white part only, thinly sliced

½ fennel bulb, thinly sliced

10 white peppercorns

6 fennel seeds

1 bay leaf

2 sprigs thyme

1 cup (250 mL) white wine

2 lb (900 g) white-fish bones, rinsed and chopped

Stems from ¼ bunch chervil

Stems from ¼ bunch parsley

2 tsp (10 mL) salt

....

In a stockpot over medium-high heat, melt butter. Add celery, onion, leek, fennel, peppercorns, fennel seeds, bay leaf, and thyme; sauté until vegetables are soft but have not started to brown, about 5 minutes.

Add wine and continue cooking until liquid has reduced by half. Add fish bones and just enough cold water to cover. Bring to a boil, then reduce heat to low and simmer for 20 minutes, skimming impurities from surface of stock as it cooks down.

Stir in herb stems and salt and simmer stock for 10 minutes more.

Strain stock through a fine-mesh sieve into a container, discarding solids. Set container of stock in kitchen sink and surround with ice water to cool as quickly as possible. Store stock in refrigerator and use within 4 days, or freeze for up to 3 months.

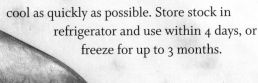

Veal Stock
Makes about 2 quarts (2 L)

....

5 lb (2.25 kg) veal bones (knuckles and shins)

3 tbsp (45 mL) canola oil

2 leeks, white and pale greens only, cut in thirds

3 onions, cut in half

4 celery stalks, cut in thirds

3 carrots, quartered

1 head of garlic, cut in half crosswise

1 cup (250 mL) water

2 tbsp (30 mL) tomato paste

½ bunch parsley

5 sprigs thyme

3 bay leaves

2 tsp (10 mL) black peppercorns

½ chopped split calf's foot

....

Preheat oven to 425°F (220°C).

Spread veal bones in a roasting pan. Drizzle with oil and toss well to coat. Roast, turning several times, until bones are golden brown, about 1 hour. Transfer bones to a stockpot and set aside.

To roasting pan, add leeks, onions, celery, carrots, and garlic; toss in the fat. Roast vegetables, tossing several times, until fork-tender, about 20 minutes.

Place roasting pan over medium heat, stir in 1 cup (250 mL) water, and deglaze pan, scraping up any brown bits stuck to the bottom. Stir in tomato paste and cook, stirring frequently, for 5 minutes.

Transfer vegetables and roasting juices to stockpot. Add enough cold water to cover vegetables and bones. Stir in parsley, thyme, bay leaves, peppercorns, and calf's foot. Bring to a boil, then reduce heat to low and simmer, uncovered, for 6 hours, skimming impurities from the surface.

Strain stock through a fine-mesh sieve into a container. Set container of stock in kitchen sink and surround with ice water to cool. Refrigerate for up to a week, or freeze for up to 3 months.

Chicken Noodle Soup

....

Who doesn't love homemade chicken noodle soup? I keep this recipe simple and lean, using chicken breasts and lots of wonderful noodles and herbs. The key to making this soup the very best? Use a real chicken stock, one that you have made, one that is rich and full of flavor. The rest is easy. *Serves 4*

....

2 tbsp (30 mL) unsalted butter

1 onion, finely chopped

1 cup (250 mL) finely chopped carrots

1 cup (250 mL) finely chopped celery

2 boneless, skinless chicken breasts

8 cups (2 L) chicken stock

1 bay leaf

1 sprig thyme

1 sprig rosemary

4 cups (1 L) cooked egg noodles

¼ cup (60 mL) chopped parsley

Salt and pepper

....

In a stockpot over medium heat, melt butter. Add onions, carrots, and celery; cook, stirring frequently, until onions are translucent, about 5 minutes. Add chicken breasts, stock, bay leaf, thyme, and rosemary. Bring to a boil, then reduce heat to low and simmer gently until chicken is cooked, about 15 minutes.

With a slotted spoon, transfer chicken to a cutting board. When cool enough to handle, cut into ½-inch (1 cm) cubes. Return to pot along with noodles and parsley and cook until heated through, about 5 minutes.

Discard bay leaf and thyme and rosemary sprigs. Season soup to taste with salt and pepper and serve immediately.

Mom's Split Pea Soup with Ham Hocks

....

I am so lucky to have not only an incredible mom but also one who really knows how to cook. One of my favorites has always been her amazing split pea soup. It's fantastic! The split peas soak up the wonderful broth, and the garnish of sour cream and green onion contrasts nicely with the soup's sweet and salty flavor and rustic texture. Now that I've started talking about it … Mom, can you make a pot now? *Serves 4*

....

3 tbsp (45 mL) unsalted butter

1 onion, finely chopped

2 cups (500 mL) diced carrots

1 cup (250 mL) diced celery

3 cloves garlic, minced

½ tsp (2 mL) red pepper flakes

1 smoked ham hock

8 cups (2 L) chicken stock

2 cups (500 mL) dried green split peas

2 bay leaves

1 sprig thyme

Salt and pepper

¼ cup (60 mL) sour cream, for garnish

1 green onion, thinly sliced, for garnish

....

In a stockpot over medium heat, melt butter. Add onions, carrots, celery, garlic, and red pepper flakes; cook, stirring frequently, until onions are translucent, about 5 minutes. Add ham hock, stock, split peas, bay leaves, and thyme. Bring to a boil, skimming off any impurities from the surface of the soup. Reduce heat to medium-low, cover, and simmer soup, stirring occasionally, until peas are very soft and meat is fall-off-the-bone tender, about 1½ hours.

Transfer ham hock to a cutting board. When cool enough to handle, discard skin and fat. Pull meat off the bone and shred. Set aside.

Discard bay leaves and thyme sprig, then use a potato masher to crush peas to desired texture. Stir in ham hock meat and season to taste with salt and pepper.

Ladle soup into warm bowls and serve garnished with a dollop of sour cream and a sprinkling of green onion.

French Onion Soup with Parmesan Garlic Bread

This soup is sophisticated, but still so much fun to eat. It's sweet and salty, with deliciously gooey cheese. The broth is crucial to the soup's success, so make sure to pay close attention in the beginning stages. Resist eating all the caramelized onions before adding the liquids. It's tough, but the long-term results are worth the wait. The cognac enhances the soup's overall nuttiness, and after all, there's nothing wrong with having some cognac lying around! For the topping, I go the extra mile and make Parmesan garlic bread. It definitely elevates this soup to the next level. This is a crowd-pleaser! *Serves 6*

....

2 tbsp (30 mL) extra-virgin olive oil

2 tbsp (30 mL) unsalted butter

2 cloves garlic, minced

6 large Vidalia onions, halved and cut in ¼-inch (5 mm) slices

3 tbsp (45 mL) granulated sugar

2 sprigs thyme

1 bay leaf

6 cups (1.5 L) beef stock

1 cup (250 mL) dry white wine

¼ cup (60 mL) cognac (optional)

Salt and pepper

Parmesan Garlic Bread (recipe follows)

8 oz (225 g) Gruyère cheese, shredded

....

In a stockpot over medium heat, heat oil and melt butter. Add garlic, onions, sugar, thyme, and bay leaf. Cook, stirring occasionally, until onions start to darken at the edges, about 15 minutes.

Reduce heat to low and leave onions to caramelize, uncovered and stirring occasionally, until bottom of the pot is covered with a rich, dark, nutty brown film, about 1 hour.

Add stock and wine; simmer for 15 minutes. (Meanwhile, make Parmesan Garlic Bread.) Stir in cognac (if using) and season to taste with salt and pepper.

Preheat broiler.

Ladle hot soup into 6 heatproof ramekins, fan 3 pieces of Parmesan garlic bread on top, and sprinkle a generous handful of Gruyère over each serving. Place ramekins on a baking sheet and broil until cheese melts and is golden, about 5 minutes. Serve immediately.

Parmesan Garlic Bread

1 baguette
½ cup (125 mL) mayonnaise
½ cup (125 mL) finely grated Parmesan cheese
2 tbsp (30 mL) minced garlic
2 tbsp (30 mL) finely chopped chives
1 tbsp (15 mL) Sriracha hot sauce

Preheat oven to 350°F (180°C).

Cut baguette into eighteen ½-inch (1 cm) slices.

In a small bowl, combine mayonnaise, Parmesan, garlic, chives, and hot sauce; stir to a smooth paste. Spread on one side of bread slices, place on a parchment-lined baking sheet, and bake until golden, about 15 minutes.

Smoked Salmon Chowder

Some of my first cooking gigs were out West in beautiful Vancouver, where I became obsessed with all the amazing fish and seafood the West Coast has to offer, always available fresh on the docks or at local fishmongers. I came up with this recipe while shooting *Pitchin' In* in the beautiful Vancouver Island town of Tofino. It's rich and smooth and packed with that distinctive smoked salmon flavor. The potatoes add substance, the leeks some sweetness, and the dill some freshness. I just love how it looks in the bowl, the broth tinged light pink from the fish, with dill and pepper spotting the top. *Serves 4 to 6*

4 tbsp (60 mL) unsalted butter
2 leeks, white part only, halved lengthwise and cut in ¼-inch (5 mm) slices
Leaves from 2 sprigs thyme
1 cup (250 mL) white wine
2 cups (500 mL) fish stock
2 cups (500 mL) heavy (35%) cream
1 lb (450 g) parboiled skin-on fingerling potatoes, cut crosswise in ¼-inch (5 mm) coins
1 cup (250 mL) smoked salmon chunks
2 tbsp (30 mL) chopped dill
Salt and pepper

In a large saucepan over medium heat, melt butter. Add leeks and cook, stirring occasionally, until softened, about 10 minutes. Stir in thyme, wine, and stock and cook for 5 minutes more.

Stir in cream and bring to a boil. Gently fold in potatoes, smoked salmon, and dill. Continue cooking until chowder is heated through, about 5 minutes. Season to taste with salt and pepper. Ladle into soup bowls and serve immediately.

Cioppino Crawford Style

This fabulous dish is another favorite from my time living on the West Coast and is perfect for sharing. It looks great and doesn't require much work. It's herbaceous, light, and filled with seafood. The clams and mussels are cooked and served in their shells, which makes for fun eating! *Serves 6*

½ cup (125 mL) unsalted butter

2 medium onions, finely chopped

3 cloves garlic, minced

Leaves from 1 bunch parsley, finely chopped

1 can (28 oz/796 mL) plum tomatoes

2 cups (500 mL) Clamato juice

1½ cups (375 mL) white wine

2 bay leaves

2 tbsp (30 mL) chopped basil

1 tsp (5 mL) chopped thyme

1 tsp (5 mL) chopped oregano

12 small hard-shell clams in shell, scrubbed

12 mussels in shell, beards removed, scrubbed

1 lb (450 g) extra-large shrimp, peeled and deveined

1 lb (450 g) bay scallops

1 lb (450 g) fish fillets (halibut, cod, salmon), cut in bite-size chunks

Salt and pepper

In a stockpot over medium-low heat, melt butter. Add onions, garlic, and parsley. Cook, stirring occasionally, until onions have softened, about 10 minutes.

Increase heat to medium-high and add tomatoes, Clamato juice, wine, bay leaves, basil, thyme, and oregano. Bring to a boil, then reduce heat to low, cover, and simmer for 30 minutes.

Gently stir in clams, mussels, shrimp, scallops, and fish fillets; cover and simmer until clams and mussels open, shrimp turn pink, and fish is opaque, about 10 minutes more.

Discard bay leaves and season cioppino to taste with salt and pepper. Ladle into soup bowls and serve immediately.

Brown Butter Crab Risotto

Risotto sounds intimidating to most home cooks, but if you can stir, you can make it. It requires constant attention, adding liquid in portions and stirring until incorporated. But its richness and incredible texture are worth the effort. *Serves 4*

········

3 cups (750 mL) fish stock
3 tbsp (45 mL) unsalted butter
1 tbsp (15 mL) olive oil
2 shallots, finely chopped
2 small Thai red chilies, thinly sliced
¾ cup (175 mL) arborio rice
¼ cup (60 mL) white wine
½ cup (125 mL) grated Parmesan cheese, plus more for garnish
½ lb (225 g) crabmeat, picked through
¼ cup (60 mL) finely chopped chives, plus more for garnish
Grated zest of ½ lemon

········

In a saucepan, bring fish stock to a simmer.

In a medium sauté pan over medium-high heat, melt butter. Add olive oil and cook until butter has browned slightly and smells nutty, about 3 minutes. Add shallots and chilies and cook, stirring frequently, until shallots are soft, about 3 minutes.

Add rice and cook, stirring, until grains are coated with butter mixture, about 3 minutes. Stir in wine and cook, stirring, until no liquid remains.

Add a ladle of hot stock and cook, stirring constantly, until the liquid is fully absorbed and rice appears almost dry. Repeat process, stirring constantly, until risotto is al dente and creamy. Total cooking time is about 25 minutes.

Remove pan from heat and gently fold in Parmesan, crab, chives, and lemon zest.

Spoon risotto into warm bowls, garnish with more cheese and chives, if desired, and serve immediately.

Fish & Chips

....

Fish and chips is a Crawford staple. I have so many happy memories of having fish and chips with my family for supper. My mom and dad both made the best chips! I am telling you, those plump, golden chips with fluffy centers and those delicious fillets of crispy, flaky fish are hands down one of my fondest food memories! This recipe is one I hope you will share with your family … something so simple is sometimes the best! *Serves 4*

....

1 lb (450 g) baking potatoes (about 3 medium), peeled
   and cut in wedges
Vegetable oil, for deep-frying
1¾ cups (425 mL) all-purpose flour, placed in freezer
   for 15 minutes before using
1 tbsp (15 mL) baking powder
2¼ cups (550 mL) very cold beer
4 skinless sustainable white-fish fillets (pollock, basa,
   tilapia, cod, halibut, etc., about 4 oz/115 g each)
Salt and pepper

....

In a large bowl, cover potatoes with cold water and let soak for an hour. Drain and pat thoroughly dry.

Preheat oven to 350°F (180°C).

In a large, deep saucepan, heat 4 inches (10 cm) oil to 330°F (165°C). Blanch potatoes in batches until barely tender, about 5 minutes. With a slotted spoon, transfer to a rack set over a baking sheet to drain.

Heat oil to 375°F (190°C). Working in batches, deep-fry potatoes a second time until crisp and golden, about 3 minutes. With a slotted spoon, transfer back to rack to drain. Keep potatoes warm in oven until ready to serve.

In another large bowl, combine chilled flour with baking powder. Slowly whisk in cold beer until batter is the consistency of smooth pancake batter.

Pat fish dry with paper towels and season to taste with salt and pepper. Working in batches, dip fillets in batter, coating well, and gently place in hot oil. Fry, turning once, until golden brown, about 4 minutes per side. With a slotted spoon, transfer fish to rack with chips in the oven. Serve fish and chips immediately with malt vinegar and tartar sauce, if desired.

Coq au Vin

This traditional French recipe might not be as fashionable as it once was, but it still tastes great and is one of my favorites. I love the classics and love their beauty of simplicity when cooking at home. I add cognac for nuttiness and lots of mushrooms for meatiness. Overall, this dish is packed with incredible flavors. It's time to bring this one back! *Serves 4*

1 chicken (about 3 lb/1.35 kg), backbone removed, cut in 8 pieces

4 cloves garlic, sliced

12 sprigs thyme

4 bay leaves

2 cups (500 mL) red wine

4 tbsp (60 mL) unsalted butter

1 cup (250 mL) finely chopped white onions

2 small plum tomatoes, diced

1 tbsp (15 mL) tomato paste

1 tsp (5 mL) thyme leaves

1 cup (250 mL) diced slab bacon

Salt and pepper

2 tbsp (30 mL) vegetable oil

1 to 2 cups (250 to 500 mL) chicken stock

¼ cup (60 mL) cognac

3 tbsp (45 mL) all-purpose flour mixed with 2 tbsp (30 mL) softened butter to form a paste

1 cup (250 mL) pearl onions, blanched and peeled

½ lb (225 g) whole button mushrooms, sautéed

½ cup (125 mL) flat-leaf parsley leaves, thinly sliced

In a large bowl, combine chicken pieces with half the garlic, 6 thyme sprigs, 2 bay leaves, and wine. Cover and refrigerate for 4 hours.

Meanwhile, in a small skillet over medium heat, melt 2 tbsp (30 mL) butter. Add chopped onions and sauté until translucent, about 10 minutes. Stir in tomatoes and tomato paste; cook, stirring frequently, for 5 minutes. Stir in thyme leaves and remaining garlic; cook 1 minute more, then remove skillet from heat and set aside.

In another small skillet over medium heat, melt remaining 2 tbsp (30 mL) butter. Add bacon and cook, stirring occasionally, until golden brown, about 15 minutes. Transfer bacon and fat to a roasting pan and set aside.

Preheat oven to 300°F (150°C).

Remove chicken from marinade (reserving marinade). Pat dry with paper towels and season to taste with salt and pepper.

In a large skillet over medium-high heat, heat vegetable oil. Working in batches, brown chicken pieces on both sides. Place on top of bacon in roasting pan. Top with reserved tomato mixture and remaining thyme sprigs and bay leaves.

Add reserved marinade to skillet and reduce by half. Skim any impurities from surface of marinade. Pour marinade over chicken. Add just enough stock to barely cover chicken.

Cover roasting pan tightly with foil and bake until chicken is tender and thoroughly cooked, about 2 hours.

With a slotted spoon, transfer chicken pieces to a platter and loosely tent with foil to keep warm.

Strain braising liquid into a saucepan, discarding solids. Add cognac and bring sauce to a boil. Whisk in just enough flour-butter paste to thicken sauce to a gravy-like consistency. Stir in pearl onions and mushrooms; cook until heated through. Spoon sauce over chicken and garnish with parsley. Serve immediately.

Fried Chicken with Lemon Thyme Honey

I serve this at just about every large gathering at my house. I love fried chicken, and so do my friends. There are never any leftovers! Fried chicken is not difficult to make. I recommend buying whole chickens and butchering them yourself. I set the chicken in the buttermilk marinade overnight to brine. This seasons the meat and helps it keep its moisture. Tossing it in seasoned flour before frying ensures that the crust will be extra-crisp. It's more likely that the fried chicken will be eaten before it gets cold, but if the impossible happens, just pop it into the oven to crisp the crust and heat it up. *Serves 4*

2 cups (500 mL) buttermilk

¼ cup (60 mL) Dijon mustard

1 tbsp (15 mL) hot sauce

2 tbsp (30 mL) onion powder

4 tsp (20 mL) salt

2 tsp (10 mL) dry mustard

2 tsp (10 mL) black pepper

1 tsp (5 mL) dried thyme

1 chicken (about 3 lb/1.35 kg), backbone removed, cut in 8 pieces

4 cups (1 L) all-purpose flour

2 tbsp (30 mL) paprika

1 tbsp (15 mL) baking powder

1 tbsp (15 mL) garlic powder

Vegetable oil, for frying

In a large resealable plastic bag, combine buttermilk, Dijon mustard, hot sauce, 1 tbsp (15 mL) onion powder, 1 tsp (5 mL) salt, 1 tsp (5 mL) dry mustard, 1 tsp (5 mL) black pepper, dried thyme, and chicken pieces. Press air from bag, seal, and refrigerate for at least 12 hours.

Preheat oven to 350°F (180°C).

In another large resealable plastic bag, mix together flour, paprika, baking powder, garlic powder, remaining 1 tbsp (15 mL) onion powder, 3 tsp (15 mL) salt, 1 tsp (5 mL) dry mustard, and 1 tsp (5 mL) black pepper.

Working in batches, remove chicken from marinade and coat in seasoned flour. Discard marinade and any leftover seasoned flour.

In a large, deep skillet over medium-high heat, heat 1¼ inches (3 cm) oil to 340°F (170°C).

Working in batches, carefully add chicken pieces skin side down to hot oil. Fry, turning once, until deep golden brown and crispy, about 10 minutes per side. Transfer chicken to a baking sheet and keep warm in oven while frying remaining pieces. Drizzle with lemon thyme honey (see page 13).

Texas-Style Chili

·········

There are so many ways to make an awesome chili. But whether you use ground meat or chuck, kidney beans or no beans at all, the basic cooking method is the same. I use chuck because I love its taste and texture. The meat starts out tough and needs time in the pot to tenderize, making the broth rich in flavor. I like my chili to have some kick, which is why I include the chipotle peppers, but feel free to use as many or as few as you like. The sugar and vinegar are added to cut the heat and lighten the chili's overall flavor. Heap it into bowls and go back for seconds! *Serves 4*

·········

¼ cup (60 mL) vegetable oil
2½ lb (1.125 kg) boneless beef chuck, well trimmed and cut in ¾-inch (2 cm) cubes
1 Spanish onion, finely chopped

4 cloves garlic, minced
4 chipotle peppers in adobo sauce, finely chopped
2 tbsp (30 mL) chili powder
1½ tsp (7 mL) ground cumin
2¼ cups (550 mL) water

2 cups (500 mL) beef stock
2 tbsp (30 mL) all-purpose flour
1 tbsp (15 mL) packed dark brown sugar
4 tsp (20 mL) white wine vinegar
Salt and pepper

·········

In a Dutch oven over medium-high heat, heat oil. Working in batches, brown beef cubes on all sides. With a slotted spoon, transfer meat to a bowl and keep warm.

Reduce heat to medium, add onions and garlic to pot, and sauté until onions are translucent, about 5 minutes. Stir in chipotles, chili powder, and cumin; cook for 2 minutes more. Stir in water and stock, then whisk in flour a little at a time to prevent lumps.

Increase heat to high. Stir in beef and any accumulated juices and bring chili to a boil, then reduce heat to low and simmer, uncovered and stirring occasionally, until meat is tender, about 2 hours.

Stir in sugar and vinegar, then season to taste with salt and pepper.

Stout-Braised Beef Stew

What better to keep you warm in the winter months? This stew has it all: substance, depth, sweetness, earthiness, and strong rustic herbs. Working in the same pot from start to finish is important. It means that all the wonderful juices from the seared meat get incorporated into the final product. The stout deglazes the pot and gives this dish its richness, working with the brown sugared onions and sweet parsnips and carrots to make each bite full and deeply satisfying. *Serves 4 to 6*

2 lb (900 g) stewing beef, cut in 1½-inch
   (4 cm) cubes

Salt and pepper

¼ cup (60 mL) olive oil

2 cups (500 mL) chopped red onions

1 tbsp (15 mL) brown sugar

2 tbsp (30 mL) chopped garlic

2 tbsp (30 mL) unsalted butter

¼ cup (60 mL) all-purpose flour

12 oz (375 mL) stout beer

2 cups (500 mL) beef stock

4 parsnips, peeled, halved lengthwise,
   and cut in 3-inch (8 cm) pieces

4 large carrots, peeled, halved lengthwise,
   and cut in 3-inch (8 cm) pieces

2 sprigs thyme

2 bay leaves

Pat beef dry and season well with salt and pepper. In a Dutch oven over medium-high heat, heat oil. Working in batches, brown beef cubes on all sides. Transfer beef to a plate and keep warm.

Reduce heat to medium-low. Add onions and brown sugar and cook, stirring occasionally, until golden, about 10 minutes. Stir in garlic and cook for 1 minute more.

Increase heat to medium-high. Add butter and, once melted, sprinkle in flour. Cook, stirring constantly, until flour has been incorporated, about 2 minutes. Stir in stout and stock, scraping up any browned bits stuck to the bottom of the pot.

Add beef and any accumulated juices. Bring to a boil, then reduce heat to medium-low. Add parsnips, carrots, thyme, and bay leaves. Cover and simmer, stirring occasionally, until beef is tender, about 30 minutes.

Uncover and continue to simmer stew until cooking liquid is thick enough to coat the back of a spoon, about 15 minutes more. Let stew rest off the heat for 5 minutes. Discard thyme sprigs and bay leaves. Season to taste with salt and pepper and serve immediately.

Mince & Tatties

Scottish for ground beef and potatoes, mince and tatties holds a special place in my heart. My parents moved to Canada from Scotland and brought with them this simple but amazingly delicious dish. Growing up, we ate it often. It was and continues to be one of my favorites. *Serves 4*

1 tbsp (15 mL) vegetable oil
1 lb (450 g) lean ground beef
2 tbsp (30 mL) unsalted butter
1 cup (250 mL) finely chopped onions
¼ cup (60 mL) all-purpose flour
3 cups (750 mL) beef stock
2 tsp (10 mL) Worcestershire sauce
1 cup (250 mL) diced carrots
1 cup (250 mL) frozen peas
Salt and pepper
4 cups (1 L) hot Whipped Potatoes (page 198)

In a large skillet over medium-high heat, heat oil. Add beef and cook, stirring frequently and breaking meat down with back of a wooden spoon, until no pink remains, about 5 minutes.

Add butter and onions and cook, stirring frequently, until browned, about 10 minutes. Sprinkle flour over mixture and cook, stirring constantly, until well incorporated, about 2 minutes more. Gradually stir in stock and Worcestershire sauce. Bring to a boil, then reduce heat to low and simmer, stirring occasionally, until gravy has thickened slightly, about 20 minutes.

Add carrots and cook until tender, about 10 minutes.

Stir in peas and cook until heated through, about 2 minutes. Season to taste with salt and pepper. Serve spooned over hot whipped potatoes.

Beef Stroganoff

For me, this dish is pure luxury. I use tenderloin for several reasons. It's lean, cooks well over high heat, *and* I believe that the gorgeous white wine and sour cream sauce deserves an equal. In the end, no matter what cut you choose, it's impossible not to fall for this dish. To make it even more tempting, I add onion rings. Their delicate, crisp texture makes these little treats a perfect match for this exceptional classic. *Serves 4*

5 tbsp (75 mL) unsalted butter

3 shallots, thinly sliced

1 lb (450 g) button mushrooms, thinly sliced

2 tbsp (30 mL) all-purpose flour

1 tbsp (15 mL) Dijon mustard

¼ cup (60 mL) white wine

1 cup (250 mL) beef stock

½ cup (125 mL) sour cream

1½ lb (675 g) beef tenderloin, cut in 3- × 1- × ⅛-inch
(8 × 2.5 cm × 3 mm) slices

Salt and pepper

2 tbsp (30 mL) finely chopped parsley

In a large saucepan over medium-high heat, melt 3 tbsp (45 mL) butter. Add shallots and mushrooms; cook, stirring frequently, until caramelized, about 10 minutes.

Sprinkle in flour and cook, stirring constantly, until well combined, about 2 minutes. Whisk in mustard and wine; reduce liquid by half.

Stir in stock, bring to a boil, and cook until thickened, about 2 minutes more. Stir in sour cream. Remove pot from heat.

In a large skillet over high heat, melt remaining 2 tbsp (30 mL) butter. Add beef and stir-fry until no pink remains, about 3 minutes. Reduce heat to low, stir in sauce, and season to taste with salt and pepper. Serve stroganoff in warmed bowls, garnished with chopped parsley.

ON THE GRILL

SALTS

Coffee Salt

Lemon Pepper Rosemary Salt

Chili Lime Salt

Flavored salts can elevate something boring into an amazing, addictive dish. The idea is simple: **salt is integral to just about every imaginable dish**, so why not turn it into its own distinctive ingredient. I'm particular about what salt I use, and prefer flaked sea salt, which doesn't have additives. So, start with salt and then use your imagination. Not only are seasoning salts an awesome addition to vegetables, meats, fishes, and even desserts, but they also make great gifts. I've included three recipes, but get creative and experiment with different herbs, spices, and other ingredients.

Coffee Salt

Makes about ½ cup (125 mL)

··········

3 tbsp (45 mL) finely ground espresso beans
1 tbsp (15 mL) black pepper
½ cup (125 mL) sea salt

··········

Mix all ingredients together. Store in an airtight container and use within 2 months.

Chili Lime Salt

Makes about ½ cup (125 mL)

··········

4 tbsp (60 mL) red pepper flakes
Grated zest of 6 limes
½ cup (125 mL) Maldon sea salt

··········

Mix all ingredients together. Store in an airtight container and use within 1 month.

Lemon Pepper Rosemary Salt

Makes about ½ cup (125 mL)

··········

¼ cup (60 mL) grated lemon zest
Leaves from 3 sprigs rosemary
1 tbsp (15 mL) black pepper
½ cup (125 mL) Maldon sea salt

··········

In a food processor, combine lemon zest, rosemary, and pepper. Process until finely chopped, about 1 minute. Add salt and pulse until mixture is well blended, about 30 seconds more.

Store in an airtight container and use within 1 month.

Rubs are more work than seasoning salts, but as a result are more complex in their flavors. **It's worth it to make your own rubs**, because the store-bought ones can be expensive and often include additives.

Rubs are primarily used on meat and fish, but I also use them to liven up sides, vegetarian and vegan dishes, as well as snacks like toasted nuts, popcorn, and chips. My Old Bay Seasoning follows the original in blending herbs and spices that go so well with fish and shellfish, and that'll have you hankering for something to drink. The Piri-Piri Chili Seasoning is all about the chili by that name, which is also known as African bird's eye chili. This seasoning originated in Portugal, and it's got heat, spice, and smokiness. The Cajun Spice is more rustic, combining sweet, smoked, spiced, and herbaceous flavors. If you like more heat, throw in some red pepper flakes.

My Old Bay Seasoning

Makes about ½ cup (125 mL)

....

2 tbsp (30 mL) celery salt

2 tsp (10 mL) ground celery seeds

2 tsp (10 mL) dry mustard

2 tsp (10 mL) black pepper

2 tsp (10 mL) sweet paprika

2 tsp (10 mL) sweet smoked paprika

1 tsp (5 mL) ground cloves

1 tsp (5 mL) ground ginger

½ tsp (2 mL) cayenne pepper

½ tsp (2 mL) ground mace

½ tsp (2 mL) ground cardamom

½ tsp (2 mL) ground allspice

....

Mix all ingredients together. Store in an airtight container and use within 2 months. Great on seafood or chicken.

Piri-Piri Chili Seasoning

Makes about ½ cup (125 mL)

....

¼ cup (60 mL) hot smoked paprika

2 tbsp (30 mL) ground piri-piri chili

2 tbsp (30 mL) salt

2 tbsp (30 mL) black pepper

2 tbsp (30 mL) onion powder

....

Mix all ingredients together. Store in an airtight container and use within 2 months.

Cajun Spice

Makes about ½ cup (125 mL)

....

2 tbsp (30 mL) sweet paprika

1 tbsp (15 mL) black pepper

1 tbsp (15 mL) kosher salt

1 tbsp (15 mL) brown sugar

2 tsp (10 mL) dried oregano

2 tsp (10 mL) dried thyme

1 tsp (5 mL) cayenne pepper

....

Mix all ingredients together. Store in an airtight container and use within 2 months.

MARINADES & SAUCES

Marinades and sauces are great to have on hand. Like salts and rubs, it's worth the effort to make these at home.

I learned this art from my dad. He was an expert at making marinades, and was especially famous for his amazing steak marinade. **Friends loved coming to our place** for summer afternoon get-togethers, and he made sure to have enough marinade on hand for everyone's meat, whether steaks, pork chops, or chicken breasts. I've used My Dad's Steak Marinade ever since. It's fantastic!

Herb Marinade
Makes about 1½ cups (375 mL)

....

¼ cup (60 mL) flat-leaf parsley leaves
¼ cup (60 mL) cilantro leaves
4 cloves garlic
2 shallots, cut in half
Juice of 1 lemon
Juice of 1 lime
2 tbsp (30 mL) sherry vinegar
¼ cup (60 mL) extra-virgin olive oil
Salt and pepper

....

In a food processor, combine parsley, cilantro, garlic, shallots, lemon and lime juice, and sherry vinegar; pulse to combine. With motor running, drizzle in oil. Season to taste with salt and pepper.

Pour into an airtight container, refrigerate, and use within 3 days.

My Dad's Steak Marinade

Makes about 1⅓ cups (325 mL)

....

½ cup (125 mL) soy sauce

⅓ cup (75 mL) olive oil

¼ cup (60 mL) balsamic vinegar

2 tbsp (30 mL) Dijon mustard

2 tbsp (30 mL) Worcestershire sauce

1 large clove garlic, grated

....

Stir all ingredients together. Pour into an airtight container, refrigerate, and use within 2 weeks.

Jerk Marinade

Makes about 1 cup (250 mL)

....

1 bunch green onions, coarsely chopped

1 or 2 Scotch bonnet peppers

¼ cup (60 mL) white vinegar

2 tbsp (30 mL) chopped fresh thyme

2 tbsp (30 mL) olive oil

1 tbsp (15 mL) brown sugar

2 tsp (10 mL) ground allspice

2 tsp (10 mL) cinnamon

2 tsp (10 mL) salt

2 tsp (10 mL) black pepper

1 tsp (5 mL) nutmeg

....

Place all ingredients in a blender and purée into a thick paste. Place in an airtight container, refrigerate, and use within 1 week.

BBQ Sauce

Makes 4 cups (1 L)

....

2 tbsp (30 mL) canola oil

2 onions, finely chopped

3 cloves garlic, grated

2 cups (500 mL) canned crushed tomatoes

1 cup (250 mL) ketchup

2 tbsp (30 mL) tomato paste

1 chipotle pepper in adobo sauce, minced

2 tbsp (30 mL) cider vinegar

2 tbsp (30 mL) Dijon mustard

¼ cup (60 mL) maple syrup

Salt and black pepper

....

In a medium saucepan, heat oil over medium heat. Add onions and garlic. Cook, stirring frequently, until onions are translucent, about 5 minutes.

Stir in tomatoes, ketchup, tomato paste, chipotle, vinegar, mustard, and maple syrup. Reduce heat to medium-low and simmer, stirring occasionally, until reduced by one-quarter, about 45 minutes.

Working in batches if necessary, purée sauce in a blender. Season to taste with salt and pepper. Pour into an airtight container, refrigerate, and use within 2 weeks.

Romesco Sauce

Makes about 2 cups (500 mL)

....

¼ cup (60 mL) olive oil

1 slice crusty bread (1 inch/2.5 cm thick), torn in pieces

½ cup (125 mL) blanched slivered almonds

4 cloves garlic, chopped

1 tsp (5 mL) salt

1 jar (8 oz/226 g) roasted red bell peppers, drained

2 cups (500 mL) canned crushed tomatoes

3 tbsp (45 mL) sherry vinegar

1 tbsp (15 mL) sweet smoked paprika

Salt and pepper

....

Preheat oven to 350°F (180°C).

In a medium skillet over medium-high heat, heat oil. Toss in bread and almonds and sauté until just beginning to brown, about 3 minutes. Add garlic and cook for 2 minutes more.

Transfer mixture to a food processor. Add salt, roasted peppers, tomatoes, vinegar, and paprika; purée until smooth. Season to taste with salt and pepper.

Spread sauce in a thin layer on a baking sheet. Bake until edges of sauce begin to caramelize, about 20 minutes.

Let sauce cool to room temperature. Spoon into an airtight container, refrigerate, and use within 1 week.

Maple Mustard BBQ Salmon

Maple and mustard are the perfect match. One's sweet and smooth and the other is hot and textured. I use them as the base for this barbecue salmon glaze, adding vinegar for some more bite, butter for richness, and thyme leaves for an aromatic finish. The result is amazing, and goes so well with the salmon's rich meat. I leave the skin on so that the meat can begin cooking before coming in contact with the barbecue's intense direct heat. Plus, the crisped skin is such a delicious treat. *Serves 4*

....

½ cup (125 mL) maple syrup

¼ cup (60 mL) whole-grain mustard

1 tbsp (15 mL) unsalted butter, melted

1 tsp (5 mL) cider vinegar

½ tsp (2 mL) finely chopped fresh thyme

Vegetable oil, for brushing

4 skin-on center-cut salmon fillets (about 6 oz/170 g each)

Salt and pepper

Maldon sea salt

....

In a small saucepan, whisk together maple syrup, mustard, butter, vinegar, and thyme. Bring to a boil over medium heat and cook for 4 minutes, stirring frequently. Remove pot from heat and set aside.

Preheat barbecue to medium-high and oil grid.

Meanwhile, brush both sides of salmon with oil and season generously with salt and pepper. Place on grid skin side down, close lid, and grill undisturbed until grill marks appear and skin is starting to crisp, about 3 minutes. Turn fillets over and brush skin side with some of the glaze. Close lid and continue to cook until salmon is opaque in the center, about 3 minutes more.

Transfer salmon to a platter and serve with remaining glaze on the side. Garnish with Maldon sea salt.

Grilled Lobster & Corn with Chipotle-Lemon Butter

For me, this dish encompasses what I love about visiting the East Coast. The fresh lobsters! The sweet corn! The beautiful coastal landscape! It feels like spritzers, summertime, and lawn chairs. This dish keeps it simple, highlighting the wonderful ingredients without much fuss. The chipotle-lemon butter gives the lobster and corn some heat and citrus. Be generous and enjoy outside. *Serves 4*

Chipotle-Lemon Butter

1 stick (½ cup/125 mL) unsalted butter, melted

1 tsp (5 mL) adobo sauce from a can of chipotle peppers in adobo

1 tsp (5 mL) grated lemon zest

2 tbsp (30 mL) lemon juice

1 tbsp (15 mL) finely chopped cilantro

1 tsp (5 mL) salt

½ tsp (2 mL) pepper

Lobsters and Sweet Corn

2 whole lobsters (about 1½ lb/675 g each)

2 ears sweet corn, shucked and cut crosswise in half

2 lemons, cut crosswise in half

½ cup (125 mL) reserved chipotle-lemon butter

For the chipotle-lemon butter, in a small bowl, stir together all ingredients. Set aside.

For the lobsters and corn, bring a large pot of water to a boil over medium-high heat. Add lobsters, cover, and cook until lobsters turn red and are almost cooked through, about 8 minutes. Immediately shock in ice water, then pat dry and cut in half lengthwise. Set aside.

Preheat barbecue to medium-high and oil grid.

Grill lobsters flesh side down for 3 minutes. Turn over, slather with chipotle-lemon butter, and grill for 3 minutes more. Transfer lobsters to a platter and keep warm.

Grill corn and lemon halves until slightly charred, about 5 minutes, brushing corn with chipotle-lemon butter several times. Serve on platter with lobster.

Grilled Jerk Chicken

....

It's not clear exactly how the term "jerk" came about, but the dish originated in Jamaica, with the indigenous Taino people, who cooked their meats over fires made from the wood of the island's allspice trees. The distinctive jerk seasoning—with allspice, hot peppers, and thyme—is essential to the dish. It has it all: heat, spice, smokiness, woodiness, and sweetness. Let the chicken marinate for about an hour so that it can absorb all the wonderful flavors. The final product is addictive, so keep the extra seasoning on hand for cravings. *Serves 4*

....

Jerk Seasoning

1 bunch green onions, coarsely chopped

1 or 2 Scotch bonnet peppers

2 tbsp (30 mL) chopped fresh thyme

1 tbsp (15 mL) brown sugar

2 tsp (10 mL) ground allspice

2 tsp (10 mL) cinnamon

2 tsp (10 mL) salt

2 tsp (10 mL) black pepper

1 tsp (5 mL) nutmeg

¼ cup (60 mL) white vinegar

2 tbsp (30 mL) olive oil

Jerk Barbecue Sauce

Juice of 1 lime

2 cups (500 mL) ketchup

2 tbsp (30 mL) honey

2 tbsp (30 mL) tamarind paste

2 tbsp (30 mL) Worcestershire sauce

1 tbsp (15 mL) jerk seasoning

1 tsp (5 mL) Dijon mustard

1 tsp (5 mL) salt

Jerk Chicken

1 chicken (about 3 lb/1.35 kg), backbone removed, cut in 8 pieces

Grated zest and juice of 1 lemon

2 tbsp (30 mL) jerk seasoning

Vegetable oil, for brushing

....

For the jerk seasoning, place all ingredients in a blender and purée into a thick paste. Spoon into an airtight container, refrigerate, and use within 5 days.

For the jerk barbecue sauce, stir all ingredients together. Pour into an airtight container, refrigerate, and use within 1 month.

For the jerk chicken, in a large bowl, toss chicken pieces with lemon zest, lemon juice, and jerk seasoning until well coated. Cover and refrigerate for 1 hour.

Preheat barbecue to medium.

Brush chicken with oil and grill for 10 minutes per side. Brush all over with some jerk barbecue sauce and continue grilling, turning occasionally, until chicken is thoroughly cooked, 15 to 20 minutes more.

Honey Whiskey Glazed Chicken

I love grilling chicken. The meat absorbs the wonderful smokiness from the grill and the flavors from the rub or marinade. Just be attentive. The breasts, which have more surface area, will finish cooking before the legs, which are thicker and contain more fat. This dish is wonderfully rustic, perfect for parties with patio lanterns.

Serves 4

....

Glaze

¾ cup (175 mL) Lemon Thyme Honey (page 13)

1 tbsp (15 mL) Sriracha hot sauce

1 tbsp (15 mL) whiskey

2 tsp (10 mL) Dijon mustard

Grated zest of 1 orange

Salt and pepper

Marinated Chicken

2 tbsp (30 mL) olive oil

2 tbsp (30 mL) whiskey

1 tsp (5 mL) Sriracha hot sauce

Juice of 1 orange

Leaves from 2 sprigs thyme

1 tsp (5 mL) salt

¼ tsp (1 mL) pepper

1 large clove garlic, grated

1 chicken (about 3 lb/1.35 kg), backbone removed, cut in 8 pieces

....

For the glaze, in a small bowl, whisk together honey, Sriracha, whiskey, mustard, and orange zest. Season to taste with salt and pepper. Set aside.

For the chicken, in a large bowl, stir together oil, whiskey, Sriracha, orange juice, thyme, salt, pepper, and garlic. Add chicken and toss well to coat. Refrigerate for 30 minutes.

Preheat barbecue to medium.

Grill chicken, turning several times, until thoroughly cooked, about 8 to 10 minutes per side, brushing chicken with glaze during last 5 minutes of grilling time.

Tandoori Chicken Legs

Indian tandoori chicken gave birth to the popular UK dish chicken tikka masala, which has since found its way to North America. I think it's worth returning to the original for its phenomenal marinade, which combines yogurt and spices. The original dish is cooked in a tandoor oven, which can reach extremely high temperatures. To simulate these temperatures, I cook it on the grill. I use chicken legs for their beautiful, tender dark meat. It's important to make small incisions in the legs before grilling to ensure that the meat on the bone gets cooked and the spices become more fully absorbed. Because the tandoori marinade can be quite hot, on the side I serve raita, which helps cool the mouth and is just so refreshing. *Serves 4*

4 whole chicken legs (about 2 lb/900 g total), skin removed

2 tbsp (30 mL) lemon juice

½ cup (125 mL) plain yogurt

3 tbsp (45 mL) vegetable oil

1 tbsp (15 mL) finely grated fresh ginger

2 cloves garlic, minced

1 tsp (5 mL) sweet paprika

1 tsp (5 mL) dry mustard

1 tsp (5 mL) kosher salt

½ tsp (2 mL) freshly ground black pepper

½ tsp (2 mL) ground cumin

½ tsp (2 mL) ground coriander

½ tsp (2 mL) turmeric

½ tsp (2 mL) nutmeg

¼ tsp (1 mL) ground cardamom

continued . . .

Using a sharp knife, make several incisions in each chicken leg, cutting right to the bone. Toss chicken with lemon juice and let sit for 5 minutes.

Meanwhile, prepare marinade by mixing together remaining ingredients. Coat chicken with marinade and refrigerate for half an hour.

Preheat barbecue to medium-high and oil grid well.

Grill chicken, turning once or twice, until no pink remains, about 15 minutes per side. Serve chicken with raita (recipe follows).

Raita
Makes about ¾ cup (175 mL)

....

½ cup (125 mL) yogurt
2 tbsp (30 mL) finely chopped cilantro
1 tbsp (15 mL) lemon juice
2 green onions, thinly sliced
⅓ cup (75 mL) grated English cucumber, squeezed dry
¼ tsp (1 mL) ground cumin
Salt and pepper

....

In a small bowl, stir together yogurt, cilantro, lemon juice, green onions, cucumber, and cumin. Season to taste with salt and pepper and refrigerate until ready to use.

Great Canadian Burger

The burger is the ultimate grilled dish. It's also a summertime staple, consumed en masse with potato salad, beers, and good friends. Everyone has their own special recipe, and mine is all about Canada: Canadian beef, Canadian Cheddar, and Canadian peameal bacon. Otherwise, I keep it simple with tomatoes, iceberg lettuce, and the usual condiments. Burgers are about being relaxed and having fun, so don't take it too seriously! *Serves 4*

....

1¾ lb (790 g) ground chuck

1 egg, beaten

2 cloves garlic, minced

Pinch of red pepper flakes

¼ cup (60 mL) finely chopped onion

2 tbsp (30 mL) chopped parsley

2 tbsp (30 mL) Dijon mustard

2 to 4 tbsp (30 to 60 mL) fresh bread crumbs

8 slices peameal bacon, cooked

4 slices aged Canadian Cheddar cheese

4 sesame hamburger buns, toasted and buttered

1 onion, cut in thick slices

8 slices tomato

4 pickles, sliced lengthwise

Iceberg lettuce leaves

Condiments of your choice (optional)

....

In a large bowl, mix together ground chuck, egg, garlic, red pepper flakes, onions, parsley, mustard, and enough bread crumbs to hold mixture together. Divide into 4 patties.

Preheat barbecue to medium-high and oil grid.

Grill patties, turning once, about 4 minutes per side for medium doneness.

Place 2 slices of peameal bacon and 1 slice of cheese on each patty, close lid, and grill until cheese melts, about 2 minutes.

Place patties in buns, garnish with onions, tomato, pickle, and iceberg lettuce, and top with condiments of your choice (if using). Serve immediately.

Dad's Steak with Red Wine Butter & Portobello Mushrooms

My dad's steak is famous. His secret? The marinade. It combines saltiness, sweetness, tanginess, and some heat, and it tastes phenomenal. I also use it to marinate the mushrooms, which act as fantastic sponges and, when served alongside the steak, really showcase the marinade's wonderful flavors. The red wine butter is pure but delicious excess. It's simple to prepare and it looks and tastes exceptional. Double the recipe, because you'll be looking for it long after the steaks have been eaten. *Serves 4*

Red Wine Butter

1 stick (½ cup/125 mL) unsalted butter,
  at room temperature
¼ cup (60 mL) red wine
2 tbsp (30 mL) minced shallot
2 tbsp (30 mL) finely chopped parsley
Salt and pepper

Marinated Steak and Mushrooms

4 New York strip steaks (about 6 oz/170 g each)
1 recipe My Dad's Steak Marinade (page 171)
4 large portobello mushrooms, cleaned
  and stems removed
Salt and pepper

For the red wine butter, cream butter with wine and shallots until smooth. Stir in parsley, season to taste with salt and pepper, and set aside.

For the steaks and mushrooms, lay steaks in a single layer in a shallow dish, spoon over half the marinade to cover both sides, and let sit at room temperature for 30 minutes.

Meanwhile, place mushrooms in a bowl and toss with remaining marinade.

Preheat barbecue to medium.

Remove steaks from marinade (discarding marinade) and barbecue, turning occasionally, for 4 minutes per side for medium-rare doneness. Transfer to a plate, tent with foil, and set aside.

Remove mushrooms from marinade (discarding marinade) and barbecue, turning once or twice, until browned, about 5 minutes.

Serve steak and mushrooms with a dollop of red wine butter on top. Season to taste with salt and pepper.

Ginger Pork Tenderloin with Grilled Pineapple

Pork tenderloin is extra lean, which is why it's important to let it marinate before cooking. This quick marinade is packed with citrus, salt, smoke, and heat. Once absorbed into the pork, its subtle flavor pairs well with the grilled pineapple, which is an easy, not to mention delicious, way to give color and even more taste to this dish. *Serves 4*

½ cup (125 mL) pineapple juice

Juice of 1 lime

¼ cup (60 mL) soy sauce

2 tsp (10 mL) sesame oil

¼ cup (60 mL) brown sugar

1 tbsp (15 mL) finely grated fresh ginger

1 tsp (5 mL) red pepper flakes

1 pork tenderloin (about 2 lb/900 g), trimmed of fat and silverskin

Salt and pepper

1 pineapple, peeled, quartered lengthwise, core removed

2 tbsp (30 mL) olive oil

In a small bowl, stir together pineapple and lime juices, soy sauce, sesame oil, brown sugar, ginger, and red pepper flakes until well combined. Pour into a large resealable plastic bag. Add pork and turn to coat with marinade. Squeeze air out of bag, seal, and marinate pork in refrigerator for 3 hours.

Preheat barbecue to medium-high and oil grid.

Remove tenderloin from marinade (discarding marinade), pat dry with paper towels, and season well with salt and pepper. Grill tenderloin over direct heat, turning several times to ensure even cooking, until an instant-read thermometer inserted in thickest part of meat registers 140°F (60°C) for medium doneness, about 25 minutes.

Transfer tenderloin to a cutting board, tent with foil, and let rest 10 minutes.

Meanwhile, brush pineapple wedges with olive oil and grill, turning, until fragrant and lightly charred on all sides, about 5 minutes.

Cut tenderloin crosswise into ½-inch (1 cm) slices. Transfer to a platter and serve immediately with grilled pineapple.

Cherry Lamb with Jeweled Rice & Charred Onion Cherry Relish

Cherry and lamb are great together. And this relish is delicious. The cherries and onions are an excellent combination, and make this dish seem extra-special. This recipe is also all about the cola, which helps brine the lamb, ensuring that the meat stays tender and moist when it's grilled. So the next time you barbecue, skip the usual suspects and go with lamb. *Serves 6*

Cherry Lamb with Jeweled Rice

3 cups (750 mL) cherry cola (or 2 cups/500 mL
   regular cola plus 1 cup/250 mL cherry juice)

3 shallots, finely chopped

4 cloves garlic, chopped

4 sprigs thyme

1 tsp (5 mL) red pepper flakes

1 tsp (5 mL) salt

½ tsp (2 mL) pepper

1 boneless butterflied leg of lamb
   (about 3 lb/1.35 kg)

2 tbsp (30 mL) olive oil

Jeweled Basmati Rice (page 203)

Charred Onion Cherry Relish

Makes about 2 cups (500 mL)

1 tbsp (15 mL) olive oil

1 tbsp (15 mL) butter

2 large onions, quartered

1 cup (250 mL) pitted fresh cherries, halved

¼ cup (60 mL) finely chopped flat-leaf parsley

Salt and pepper

In a large bowl, stir together cola, shallots, garlic, thyme, red pepper flakes, salt, and pepper. Add lamb, turning to coat, then cover and refrigerate for 2 hours to marinate.

For the Charred Onion Cherry Relish, in a large skillet over medium-high heat, heat oil and melt butter. Add onions and cook, stirring occasionally, until dark golden brown, about 15 minutes.

Add cherries and cook until tender, about 5 minutes. Stir in parsley and season to taste with salt and pepper. Remove from heat. Serve at room temperature.

Preheat barbecue to medium.

Remove lamb from marinade (discarding marinade) and pat dry. Rub both sides with oil. Grill lamb about 10 minutes per side for medium-rare doneness.

Let lamb rest for 10 minutes before slicing. Serve with jeweled basmati rice and onion cherry relish.

Grilled Chorizo Sausage with Queso Fresco & Lemon Aïoli

Queso fresco is a delicious fresh Mexican cheese. Its flavor is fresh, bright, milky, and mild. But it provides a nice contrast to the spicy sausage. Serve this dish on a large platter. It's colorful and filled with great textures. *Serves 4*

1 red bell pepper, cut crosswise in ¼-inch (5 mm) rings

1 yellow bell pepper, cut crosswise in ¼-inch (5 mm) rings

1 red onion, cut crosswise in ½-inch (1 cm) slices

2 tbsp (30 mL) olive oil

Salt and freshly ground pepper

4 fresh chorizo sausages

¾ cup (175 mL) queso fresco cheese

¼ cup (60 mL) cilantro leaves, for garnish

Lemon aïoli

Lemon Aïoli
Makes about 1 cup (250 mL)

¾ cup (175 mL) mayonnaise

1 tbsp (15 mL) finely grated lemon zest

1 tbsp (15 mL) lemon juice

2 tsp (10 mL) Dijon mustard

1 clove garlic, minced

Salt and ground pepper

For the lemon aïoli, in a small bowl, whisk together mayonnaise, lemon zest and juice, mustard, and garlic until well combined, then season to taste with salt and pepper. Refrigerate until ready to serve.

Preheat barbecue to medium-high.

In a large bowl, toss together peppers, onions, and olive oil. Season to taste with salt and pepper. Set aside.

Grill chorizo until thoroughly cooked, about 15 minutes, turning often to ensure even browning. Transfer sausages to a platter.

Grill peppers and onion slices, turning often, until tender and slightly charred, about 5 minutes. Place on top of sausages and garnish with queso fresco and cilantro. Serve with lemon aïoli.

Grilled Flatbread with Parsley Pesto, Tomato & Goat Cheese

I love this flatbread recipe. The dough bubbles up quickly from the heat and the grill leaves beautiful markings. This dish is fresh and colorful. The parsley pesto is so refreshing. It is absorbed into the dough, infusing it with wonderful flavors, and lays the foundation for the tomatoes as well as the arugula and goat cheese topping. Don't be intimidated about making your own dough. It's so simple and satisfying. This dish is uncomplicated and plain delicious. *Serves 4*

Flatbread

1 cup (250 mL) lukewarm water
1 tbsp (15 mL) active dry yeast
1 tbsp (15 mL) honey
2½ cups (625 mL) all-purpose flour
1 tsp (5 mL) salt
¼ cup (60 mL) olive oil

Parsley Pesto

2 cups (500 mL) parsley leaves and tender stems
1 clove garlic
¼ cup (60 mL) extra-virgin olive oil
Salt and pepper

To assemble

4 cups (1 L) tri-colored cherry tomatoes, halved
2 tbsp (30 mL) extra-virgin olive oil
2 cups (500 mL) arugula
6 oz (170 g) soft goat cheese

For the flatbread, in a medium bowl, stir together water, yeast, and honey. Let sit until mixture is frothy, about 10 minutes.

In a large bowl, stir together flour and salt. Pour in oil and yeast mixture and stir into a smooth dough. Cover and let rise until doubled in size, about 1 hour.

Meanwhile, make the parsley pesto. In a blender, purée parsley, garlic, and oil. Season to taste with salt and pepper.

Preheat barbecue or griddle to medium.

Cut dough into 4 portions and roll each piece out on a lightly floured work surface to a ¼-inch (5 mm) thickness.

Grill flatbreads for 2 minutes per side.

To assemble, toss tomatoes with oil and season to taste with salt and pepper. Smear pesto on warm flatbreads, top with tomatoes, then garnish with arugula and goat cheese. Serve immediately.

Grilled Cauliflower Steak with Summer Ratatouille Relish

....

The grill is so meat focused sometimes, I wanted to share one of Ruby Watchco's most popular vegetarian favorites. Vegetables are so versatile and fantastic, so it's not that difficult to imagine them as an entrée. The cauliflower steak is accompanied by a wonderful relish that is packed with different flavors. I love how it all comes together— the juices from the vegetables get absorbed into the pearl-like Israeli couscous, making each bite equally exciting. *Serves 4*

1 large head cauliflower, cut crosswise
    into 4 "steaks" 1 inch (2.5 cm) thick
1 zucchini, halved lengthwise
1 red bell pepper, halved lengthwise
1 yellow bell pepper, halved lengthwise
2 green onions
4 tbsp (60 mL) olive oil
Salt and pepper

¾ cup (175 mL) cherry tomatoes, halved
2 tbsp (30 mL) finely chopped basil
2 tbsp (30 mL) pitted black olives, finely chopped
1 tbsp (15 mL) capers, finely chopped
1 tbsp (15 mL) balsamic vinegar
2 cups (500 mL) cooked Israeli couscous
¼ cup (60 mL) Brown Derby Vinaigrette (page 60)

· · · · · · · · · ·

Preheat barbecue to medium-high.

Starting near base, cut four ½-inch (1 cm) crosswise slices from cauliflower. Set aside.

Lightly brush zucchini, peppers, and green onions with 1 tbsp (15 mL) oil, then season to taste with salt and pepper. Grill, turning frequently, until fork-tender and slightly charred, about 10 minutes. Remove vegetables from grill and reduce heat to medium.

When vegetables are cool enough to handle, cut into small dice. Place in a bowl along with tomatoes, basil, olives, capers, and balsamic vinegar. Toss well to combine. Set aside relish.

Brush both sides of cauliflower steaks with remaining 3 tbsp (45 mL) of oil and grill over medium indirect heat with the lid down, turning only once, until fork-tender, about 8 minutes per side.

Spoon couscous onto a platter, fan cauliflower steaks over top, then drizzle with vinaigrette. Spoon ratatouille relish over cauliflower. Serve immediately.

ON THE SIDE

Whipped Potatoes

....

I could eat potatoes every day. When I was young, it was my job to peel the potatoes and get them on the stove. If you don't have a ricer, just mash the potatoes while adding the cream mixture. I use leftover whipped potatoes to make Tattie Scones (page 53) the next morning. *Serves 4*

....

2 lb (900 g) russet potatoes, peeled and quartered
½ cup (125 mL) heavy (35%) cream
½ cup (125 mL) milk
3 tbsp (45 mL) unsalted butter
Salt and pepper

....

Place potatoes in a pot of cold salted water and bring to a boil. Reduce heat to medium-low and simmer until fork-tender, about 20 minutes.

Meanwhile, in another large saucepan over medium heat, heat cream, milk, and butter until butter has melted. Keep warm.

Drain potatoes well, then force through a ricer into warm cream mixture. Stir to combine, then season to taste with salt and pepper. Serve immediately.

Thyme & Garlic Roasted Potatoes

....

Any kind of potato will do in this dish. They are simply roasted with lots of garlic, thyme, and olive oil. Golden brown and crisp on the outside, hot and fluffy on the inside … a perfect side for any dish! *Serves 4*

....

2 Yukon Gold potatoes, scrubbed, patted dry, and cut in ¼-inch (5 mm) rounds
2 large red potatoes, scrubbed, patted dry, and cut in ¼-inch (5 mm) rounds
6 sprigs thyme
3 cloves garlic, smashed
3 tbsp (45 mL) olive oil
1 tsp (5 mL) salt
½ tsp (2 mL) cracked black pepper

....

Preheat oven to 400°F (200°C).

In a large bowl, combine potatoes, thyme, garlic, oil, salt, and pepper; toss well to coat. Spread in a single layer on a baking sheet and roast, tossing occasionally to ensure even browning, until potatoes are fork-tender and golden brown, about 25 minutes. Serve immediately.

Scalloped Potatoes

This is the dish that people keep coming back to even after dessert. No doubt the Gruyère is to blame. Crisped on top of the potatoes, its saltiness complements the rich sauce. But don't hesitate to use other hard cheeses, such as Thunder Oak Gouda, Emmental, or Parmesan. The result will be just as delicious. *Serves 6*

....

6 large waxy potatoes, peeled and cut in
⅛-inch (3 mm) rounds
1¼ cups (300 mL) heavy (35%) cream
1 tsp (5 mL) finely chopped garlic
1 tsp (5 mL) salt
½ tsp (2 mL) cracked black pepper
Pinch of freshly grated nutmeg
1 tbsp (15 mL) unsalted butter, cut in small cubes
1 cup (250 mL) shredded Gruyère cheese

....

Preheat oven to 350°F (180°C). Generously grease a 2-quart (2 L) gratin dish or 8-inch (2 L) square glass baking dish.

In a large bowl, combine potatoes, cream, garlic, salt, pepper, and nutmeg; toss well to coat. Turn potato mixture into gratin dish. Dot with butter and sprinkle cheese on top.

Cover with foil and bake for 1 hour. Remove foil and continue baking until potatoes are golden brown, about 10 minutes more. Serve immediately.

Potato Rösti

These potato cakes are so simple to make and look fantastic. The röstis' crisp skirts are elegant and the final product delicious. Make sure to let them get nice and brown. It's the crisp, slightly caramelized exterior that keeps them together and enhances their flavor. *Serves 4*

....

2 lb (900 g) russet potatoes, peeled
1 tbsp (15 mL) salt
2 tbsp (30 mL) canola oil
2 tbsp (30 mL) unsalted butter

....

Preheat oven to 200°F (100°C).

On the large holes of a box grater, grate potatoes into a large bowl. Stir in salt and let sit for 2 minutes. Squeeze out excess liquid and shape potatoes into 4 cakes.

In a large skillet over medium-low heat, heat oil and melt butter. Add 2 potato cakes and, using a metal spatula, gently press cakes down until ¼ inch (5 mm) thick. Cook, turning once, until golden, about 5 minutes per side. Transfer rösti to a baking sheet and keep warm in the oven. Repeat with remaining cakes. Keep warm in oven until ready to serve.

Potato Rösti

Scalloped Potatoes

Thyme & Garlic
Roasted Potatoes

Whipped Potatoes

Jeweled Basmati Rice

This dish is the king of rices and the rice of kings. *Serves 4 to 6*

1 tbsp (15 mL) olive oil

1 cup (250 mL) basmati rice, rinsed several
   times in cold water and well drained

½ cup (125 mL) sun-dried cherries

1 tsp (5 mL) salt

½ tsp (2 mL) pepper

¼ tsp (1 mL) ground ginger

Pinch of saffron threads

2 cups (500 mL) chicken stock

½ cup (125 mL) slivered almonds, toasted

2 green onions, thinly sliced

¼ cup (60 mL) finely chopped parsley

In a medium saucepan over medium heat, combine oil, rice, cherries, salt, pepper, ginger, and saffron. Stir-fry for 5 minutes. Stir in stock, bring to a boil, then reduce heat to low, cover, and cook until all the liquid is absorbed and rice is al dente, about 15 minutes.

Stir in almonds, green onions, and parsley and serve immediately.

Curried Lentils

Lentils are so versatile and substantial. They make an excellent base for so many wonderful dishes, but can also stand on their own. Ras el hanout is an aromatic Moroccan spice and herb blend that can contain up to 35 ingredients, depending on the spice blender's unique recipe. It gives these lentils an extra-complex and warm flavor. *Serves 4*

....

1 tsp (5 mL) olive oil
3 tbsp (45 mL) butter
2 cups (500 mL) cooked lentils
2 tsp (10 mL) ras el hanout
½ cup (125 mL) chicken stock
Salt and pepper
Cilantro leaves and Greek yogurt, for garnish

....

In a medium skillet over medium-high heat, heat oil and melt butter. Add lentils, ras el hanout, and stock; cook, stirring frequently, until liquid has reduced by half, about 5 minutes. Season to taste with salt and pepper.

Transfer lentils to a serving dish, sprinkle with cilantro leaves, and top with a few dollops of yogurt. Serve immediately.

Slow Baked Beans with Maple Syrup

These beans serve up Canadian comfort at its best. With the maple and bacon additions, this recipe boasts Canada's most famous home-grown ingredients. Enjoy with just about anything and anyone. *Serves 4*

1 tbsp (15 mL) olive oil

1 tbsp (15 mL) butter

2 slices bacon, diced

1 medium carrot, finely chopped

1 stalk celery, finely chopped

½ cup (125 mL) finely chopped onion

2 tbsp (30 mL) tomato paste

1 fresh bay leaf

2 sprigs thyme

2 cups (500 mL) cooked white navy beans

1 cup (250 mL) chicken stock

¼ cup (60 mL) maple syrup

In a medium saucepan over medium-high heat, heat oil and melt butter. Add bacon, carrot, celery, and onions; sauté until onions are translucent, about 5 minutes.

Add tomato paste, bay leaf, and thyme; cook for 2 minutes, stirring frequently. Stir in beans, stock, and maple syrup, reduce heat to low, and simmer until sauce has thickened, about 10 minutes more. Discard bay leaf and serve beans immediately.

Heirloom Carrots with Honey Thyme Butter

....

Heirloom carrots turn this simple dish into something special. Their beautiful colors—yellow, purple, and red—and varied shapes make for an attractive dish, while the honey thyme butter is delicate, sweet, and smooth. *Serves 4*

....

1 bunch heirloom carrots (about 5 carrots),
   peeled and cut in ¼-inch (5 mm) rounds.
1 tsp (5 mL) olive oil
1 tbsp (15 mL) butter
1 tbsp (15 mL) honey
Leaves from 5 sprigs thyme

....

Half fill a medium saucepan with water and bring to a boil. Add carrots and blanch for 3 minutes. Drain well. Spread in a single layer on a rimmed baking sheet to cool slightly.

In a medium skillet over medium-high heat, heat oil and melt butter. Add honey, carrots, and thyme; sauté until tender-crisp, about 5 minutes. Serve immediately.

Heirloom Carrots with Honey Thyme Butter

Espelette-Roasted Butternut Squash

Espelette-Roasted Butternut Squash

I've always been drawn to the Espelette, France's very own chili. Its subtle, sweet heat is wonderful with all vegetables, and in this case, brilliant with butternut squash. *Serves 4*

1 butternut squash (about 3 lb/1.35 kg), halved lengthwise, seeded, and cut in small wedges
2 tbsp (30 mL) olive oil
1 tsp (5 mL) salt
¼ tsp (1 mL) Espelette pepper
¼ tsp (1 mL) smoked paprika

Preheat oven to 400°F (200°C).

In a large bowl, combine squash, oil, salt, Espelette, and paprika; toss until well coated. Spread in a single layer on a baking sheet and roast until fork-tender, about

Kale with Sweet & Smoky Mustard

Charred Broccoli with Lemon Garlic Butter

Charred Broccoli with Lemon Garlic Butter

I love charred vegetables! Charring adds an amazing smoky flavor to the broccoli, which is then balanced with the fresh and punchy lemon garlic butter. Use this butter generously. *Serves 4*

2 cups (500 mL) broccoli florets
2 tbsp (30 mL) olive oil
2 tbsp (30 mL) butter
1 clove garlic, minced
Grated zest of ½ lemon
1 tbsp (15 mL) lemon juice
Salt and pepper

Preheat oven to 400°F (200°C).

Toss broccoli with oil to coat. Spread in a single layer on a baking sheet and roast, turning once, just until tender and slightly charred, about 15 minutes.

Meanwhile, in a small saucepan over medium heat, melt butter. Stir in garlic and lemon zest and cook for 1 minute. Remove from heat and whisk in lemon juice. Season to taste with salt and pepper.

In a large bowl, toss broccoli in lemon butter sauce to coat. Serve immediately.

Kale with Sweet & Smoky Mustard

I think that mustard is the perfect addition to just about any dish. In this recipe, I use two different kinds, for flavor and texture. The robust kale leaves are strong enough to carry the rich reduced sauce. Dress the dish with as much or as little sauce as you want, or drizzle it over your main. I think pork chops are especially nice here. *Serves 4*

1 tbsp (15 mL) olive oil
1 bunch kale, stems removed, leaves shredded
⅔ cup (150 mL) water
2 tbsp (30 mL) sherry vinegar
2 tsp (10 mL) packed brown sugar
2 tsp (10 mL) whole-grain mustard
2 tsp (10 mL) sweet and smoky mustard
1 tsp (5 mL) salt

In a medium skillet over medium heat, heat oil. Add kale and sauté for 1 minute, then add water and cook, stirring occasionally, until kale is tender and most of the water has evaporated, about 3 minutes.

Stir in vinegar, brown sugar, mustards, and salt. Increase heat to high and cook, stirring frequently, for 2 minutes more.

Using a slotted spoon, transfer kale to a serving dish. Place skillet back on heat and reduce cooking liquid by half, about 3 minutes. Pour over kale and serve immediately.

Brussels Sprouts with Bacon

This dish will redeem Brussels sprouts for all kids! Not hard to do when you just add some bacon and cook until the sprouts' edges have caramelized. The bacon fat helps bring out the sprouts' natural sweetness. I like mine to still be firm, but don't hesitate to cook longer if you want your Brussels to continue softening and sweetening.

Serves 4

....

6 slices thick bacon, sliced crosswise in ¼-inch (5 mm) pieces

1 lb (450 g) Brussels sprouts, trimmed and halved lengthwise

Salt and pepper

....

In a large skillet over medium-high heat, cook bacon until fat has rendered and bacon is crispy, about 5 minutes. With a slotted spoon, transfer bacon to paper towels to drain.

To fat in skillet, add sprouts and cook, stirring occasionally, until caramelized, about 10 minutes.

Return bacon to skillet, season to taste with salt and pepper, and serve immediately.

Roasted Cauliflower

. . . .

Roasted cauliflower is so delicious. It becomes tender and the florets caramelize. I love the little crisped bits that end up in the pan. They're a nice contrast to the sweetened, plumped raisins. This dish is loaded with rich, textured flavors. *Serves 4*

. . . .

1 large head cauliflower, broken into florets
Grated zest and juice of 1 lemon
Leaves from 2 sprigs rosemary, coarsely chopped
2 tbsp (30 mL) seedless raisins
2 tbsp (30 mL) olive oil
2 tbsp (30 mL) butter, melted
1 tsp (5 mL) ground cumin
1 tsp (5 mL) salt
½ tsp (2 mL) cracked black pepper
Chopped parsley, for garnish

. . . .

Preheat oven to 400°F (200°C).

In a large bowl, combine cauliflower, lemon zest and juice, rosemary, raisins, oil, butter, cumin, salt, and pepper; toss to coat.

Spread in a single layer on a parchment-lined baking sheet and roast, tossing halfway through, until golden brown and crispy, about 30 minutes. Sprinkle with parsley and serve immediately.

Roasted Cauliflower

Brussels Sprouts
with Bacon

Creamed Mushrooms with Parmesan

These creamed mushrooms are fabulous in the colder months—or any months, really! The Parmesan cream sauce is so delicious. I leave the mushrooms whole. I love how it looks, and the mushrooms pop in your mouth! *Serves 4*

Red Wine Braised Onions

Creamed Mushrooms with Parmesan

1 tsp (5 mL) vegetable oil
2 tbsp (30 mL) butter
1 lb (450 g) white mushrooms, stems removed
½ cup (125 mL) heavy (35%) cream
½ cup (125 mL) grated Parmesan cheese
Salt and pepper
Finely chopped parsley, for garnish

In a medium skillet over medium-high heat, heat oil and melt butter. Add mushrooms and cook, stirring frequently, until golden brown, about 8 minutes.

Stir in cream and Parmesan and continue cooking until sauce thickens enough to coat the back of a spoon, about 6 minutes more. Season to taste with salt and pepper, garnish with parsley, and serve immediately.

Red Wine Braised Onions

For the smell alone! The vinegar reduces and the onions caramelize, producing an irresistible sweetness and subtle tanginess. Don't be afraid to play around with the size of your onions. Smaller rings also make for an excellent garnish. These onions are simple, but perfect for any meal. *Serves 4*

1 tbsp (15 mL) packed brown sugar
1 tsp (5 mL) salt
1 tsp (5 mL) olive oil
2 medium red onions, cut in ½-inch (1 cm) rounds
¼ cup (60 mL) red wine
3 tbsp (45 mL) sherry vinegar
4 tsp (20 mL) butter

In a large skillet over medium heat, stir together sugar, salt, and oil to combine. Add onions and, being careful to keep rounds intact, sauté until caramelized, about 3 minutes per side. Stir in red wine, vinegar, and butter and cook until sauce is reduced by half, about 3 minutes more.

Transfer onion rounds to a serving dish, drizzle with pan juices, and serve immediately.

Prosciutto-Wrapped Asparagus

This dish is simple but always popular. I like using very thinly sliced prosciutto so that it almost seals onto the asparagus in the heat. Cook until the prosciutto is crisp and the asparagus is bright green. Serve while hot and the color still pops. *Serves 4*

....

1 lb (450 g) asparagus, trimmed
4 oz (115 g) thinly sliced prosciutto
2 tsp (10 mL) olive oil

....

Working on a slight diagonal, wrap a slice of prosciutto around a spear of asparagus, leaving asparagus tip exposed. Repeat with remaining prosciutto and asparagus.

In a medium skillet over medium heat, heat oil. Working in batches, cook asparagus, turning occasionally, until spears turn bright green and prosciutto is crisp, about 5 minutes. Serve immediately.

Yorkshire Puddings

Don't be fooled—Yorkshire puddings are simple to make. Just be sure that your pan is smoking hot and that you don't open the oven while the puddings are rising. Abide by these two basic rules and you'll be impressing guests with these light and doughy delights. *Makes 12 puddings*

4 large eggs
1 cup (250 mL) whole (3.25%) milk
1 cup (250 mL) all-purpose flour
1 tsp (5 mL) salt
¼ cup (60 mL) vegetable oil or beef drippings

Set a rack in upper third of oven and preheat oven to 425°F (220°C).

In a medium bowl, whisk together eggs, milk, flour, and salt until smooth. Set aside.

Place 1 tsp (5 mL) oil or beef drippings into each cup of a 12-cup muffin pan. Transfer pan to oven and heat until oil is smoking, about 2 minutes.

Remove pan from oven and quickly pour batter into cups, filling three-quarters full. Bake until puddings have risen and are golden brown, about 15 minutes. Serve immediately.

EAT, DRINK & GET HAPPY

The Pitchin' In

....

I served this drink to guests at the launch for my first cookbook and it's been in high demand at the restaurant ever since. Warning: the brown butter rim is seriously good. *Serves 1*

....

Ginger Syrup

Makes enough for 8 drinks

½ cup (125 mL) granulated sugar

½ cup (125 mL) water

½-inch (1 cm) piece fresh ginger, peeled and thinly sliced

Carrot Purée

Makes enough for 4 drinks

1 carrot, thinly sliced

1 tsp (5 mL) granulated sugar

....

To assemble

1 tsp (5 mL) brown butter, melted

1 tbsp (15 mL) Demerara sugar

2 oz (60 mL) apple cider

1½ oz (45 mL) Sailor Jerry spiced rum

2 tbsp (30 mL) carrot purée

1 tbsp (15 mL) ginger syrup

1 tbsp (15 mL) fresh lime juice

For the ginger syrup, in a medium saucepan, stir together sugar, water, and ginger. Bring to a boil over medium-high heat and cook until sugar has dissolved. Reduce heat to low and simmer for 5 minutes more. Remove pan from heat and let mixture steep for 1 hour.

Pour through a fine-mesh sieve into an airtight container and refrigerate for up to 1 month.

For the carrot purée, place carrots and sugar in a small saucepan, cover with water, bring to a boil over medium-high heat, and cook until carrots are fork-tender, about 10 minutes.

With a slotted spoon, transfer carrots to a blender. Process with just enough cooking liquid to achieve a smooth purée. Cool slightly, then pour into an airtight container and refrigerate until ready to use.

Rim a chilled cocktail glass with brown butter and Demerara sugar. In a cocktail shaker filled with ice, combine cider, rum, carrot purée, ginger syrup, and lime juice. Shake until frothy, then strain into glass. Serve immediately.

The Boultbee Bourbon

I love thinking up new drinks for at-home parties with friends. This one's fun and fresh. The blackberries add tartness to the maple syrup. Bourbon rounds out this drink with a fresh citrus twist. I prefer Woodford Reserve bourbon, but use your own favorite. *Serves 1*

4 blackberries
1 orange wedge
1½ oz (45 mL) bourbon
4 tsp (20 mL) fresh lemon juice
4 tsp (20 mL) maple syrup
2 oz (60 mL) club soda

In a cocktail shaker, muddle together 3 blackberries and orange wedge. Fill shaker with ice, then add bourbon, lemon juice, and maple syrup. Shake well.

Strain into an ice-filled rocks glass and stir in club soda. Garnish with remaining blackberry and serve immediately.

The Boultbee
Bourbon

3 G's

Alex in
Wonderland

The NYC Bicycle

The Pitchin' In

The NYC Bicycle

This drink is perfect for enjoying at the cottage during those hot summer days. It's fresh and effervescent and will have you doing cartwheels in no time. Just ask Tommy and Lora!

Serves 1

5 mint leaves
1½ oz (45 mL) gin
⅔ cup (150 mL) sparkling grapefruit soda
   such as San Pellegrino Pompelmo
Lime wedge, for garnish

In a cocktail shaker, muddle mint leaves with gin. Fill shaker with ice, shake well, then strain into a chilled highball glass. Add soda and stir briefly. Garnish with lime wedge and serve immediately.

3 G's

This cocktail was created with my friend Karla from Brooklyn, New York. Karla flew up to give us a hand for the opening of my restaurant, Ruby Watchco. She created lots of delicious cocktails, but this one is one of my favorites. The ginger beer adds spice and sweetness. Candied ginger makes for an awesome and fitting garnish. This drink has become a classic and has not left the menu yet!

Serves 1

1½ oz (45 mL) gin
2 oz (60 mL) freshly squeezed orange juice
1 tsp (5 mL) lime juice
1 tbsp (15 mL) ginger syrup (page 224)
2 oz (60 mL) ginger beer
Orange slice, for garnish
Crystallized ginger, for garnish

In a cocktail shaker filled with ice, combine gin, orange juice, lime juice, and ginger syrup. Shake for 10 seconds, then strain into a cocktail glass filled with ice. Stir in ginger beer. Garnish with orange slice and candied ginger and serve immediately.

Alex in Wonderland

By definition this is a Negroni, the Italian classic. But let's just say that the cookbook wouldn't have been the same without it. On one particular post-work evening spent with the team at the photo shoot for this chapter, we all chose a drink to try. Well, after tumbling down the rabbit hole, drinks in hand, and after many laughs, we all named this one after Alex! *Serves 1*

1 oz (30 mL) Campari
1 oz (30 mL) gin
1 oz (30 mL) sweet vermouth
Orange peel, for garnish

Fill a rocks glass with ice, add Campari, gin, and vermouth, and stir to combine. Garnish with a strip of orange peel and serve immediately.

Caesar with Maple Bacon Jerky & a Pickle

This drink is all you need to get going after one too many Alex in Wonderlands (page 229). The jerky and pickle pretty much make this a meal. It's spicy and substantial, perfect for a Sunday brunch. *Serves 1*

Lemon wedge

Celery salt

1½ oz (45 mL) vodka

1½ tsp (7 mL) lemon juice

1 tsp (5 mL) grated fresh horseradish

3 dashes Worcestershire sauce, or to taste

2 dashes hot sauce, or more to taste

½ cup (125 mL) Clamato juice

Freshly ground black pepper

1 celery stalk with leaves, for garnish

1 dill pickle, for garnish

1 slice Maple Bacon Jerky, for garnish (page 236)

Rim a highball glass with lemon wedge and celery salt. Fill with ice, then add vodka, lemon juice, horseradish, Worcestershire sauce, hot sauce, and Clamato juice. Stir, then season to taste with pepper and celery salt. Garnish with celery stalk, pickle, and bacon jerky and serve immediately.

Bubbles

What can I say? This drink is as simple as chilling the bottle and popping the top. I include it because sometimes it's all you need. And let's face it, you probably deserve it. Right?

Serves 4

....

1 bottle really good champagne
A bucket of ice

....

Chill champagne bottle in a bucket of ice for 30 minutes. Remove wire cage, place a towel over top of cork, and gently twist it back and forth to remove.

Serve champagne in stemmed flutes; admire the flow of bubbles to the crown of the glass. And the champagne's delicious aromas. Raise your glass, sip, and enjoy!

SANGRIA

Sangria is for summer! … and spring … and probably also the fall. **Serve in big glass pitchers** or bowls to feature all the beautiful colors. I like to macerate a small portion of the ingredients to enhance the flavor.

Sparkling Pineapple Orange Sangria

Serves 6 to 8

1 bottle (750 mL) white wine, such as Riesling
¾ cup (175 mL) peach vodka
1 cup (250 mL) pineapple juice
½ cup (125 mL) honey
1 small orange, quartered and thinly sliced
1 cup (250 mL) diced fresh pineapple
Club soda

In a large pitcher, stir together wine, vodka, pineapple juice, and honey until combined, then add orange and pineapple pieces. Refrigerate for at least 1 hour.

Pour sangria into ice-filled glasses, top off with a splash of club soda, and garnish with some of the sangria fruit. Serve immediately.

Strawberry Melon Sangria

Serves 6 to 8

1 bottle (750 mL) dry red wine, such as Chianti
¼ cup (60 mL) brandy
¼ cup (60 mL) orange liqueur, such as Cointreau
¼ cup (60 mL) honey
1 cup (250 mL) thinly sliced strawberries
1 cup (250 mL) finely diced cantaloupe
1 lemon, thinly sliced
Mint leaves

In a large pitcher, stir together wine, brandy, orange liqueur, and honey until well combined, then add strawberry slices and diced melon. Refrigerate for at least 1 hour.

Pour sangria into ice-filled glasses and garnish with some of the sangria fruit, lemon slices, and mint leaves. Serve immediately.

Maple Bacon Jerky

The holy trinity: salts, sweets, and bacon. Make in advance and keep on hand. It stores well, and I promise that all mouths will gravitate towards this treat, again and again. *Makes 24 pieces*

....

½ cup (125 mL) packed light brown sugar

2 tbsp (30 mL) maple syrup

2 tsp (10 mL) chili powder

1 tsp (5 mL) freshly cracked black pepper

24 slices thick-cut bacon

Maldon sea salt

....

Preheat oven to 400°F (200°C).

In a small bowl, whisk together sugar, maple syrup, chili powder, and pepper until well combined.

Set a wire rack inside a foil-lined baking sheet. Arrange bacon in a single layer on rack and coat with sugar mixture.

Roast bacon until almost crisp, about 20 minutes. Let cool to room temperature before serving. Garnish with Maldon sea salt.

Warm Spiced Olives

I love olives warmed and spiced. Through heating, the olives become tender and juicy, highlighting their delicious saltiness. It's an easy way to liven up this favorite snack. *Makes 2 cups (500 mL)*

2 cups (500 mL) mixed olives, rinsed and patted dry

Peel of 1 lemon, cut in 2- × ½-inch (5 × 1 cm) strips

Peel of 1 orange, cut in 2- × ½-inch (5 × 1 cm) strips

½ cup (125 mL) extra-virgin olive oil

3 cloves garlic, smashed

3 sprigs thyme, cut in 1-inch (2.5 cm) pieces

1 sprig rosemary, cut in 1-inch (2.5 cm) pieces

2 bay leaves

1 tsp (5 mL) red pepper flakes

1 tsp (5 mL) fennel seeds, crushed

Place olives, lemon peel, and orange peel in a medium bowl.

In a small saucepan, combine oil, garlic, thyme, rosemary, bay leaves, red pepper flakes, and fennel seeds. Cook over low heat, stirring occasionally, until fragrant, about 10 minutes. Pour oil mixture over olives and stir to coat. Let olives marinate at room temperature for 2 hours.

Reheat olives over low heat and serve immediately or spoon into an airtight container and refrigerate until ready to use.

Bacon Peanut Brittle

Call this breakfast. It was ours, with coffees and teas each morning before starting work on this cookbook. The bacon adds a subtle saltiness to the sweet brittle. It's seriously addictive. *Makes about 1 lb (450 g)*

1 cup (250 mL) granulated sugar
½ cup (125 mL) light corn syrup
¼ cup (60 mL) water
½ tsp (2 mL) sea salt
1 cup (250 mL) unsalted roasted peanuts
½ cup (125 mL) finely chopped crispy cooked bacon
¼ tsp (1 mL) red pepper flakes
2 tbsp (30 mL) unsalted butter
1 tsp (5 mL) baking soda

Set a well-greased baking sheet in the oven and preheat oven to 300°F (150°C).

In a large saucepan, combine sugar, corn syrup, water, and salt. Stir over medium heat until sugar has dissolved. Stir in peanuts, bacon, and red pepper flakes and cook, stirring frequently, until mixture registers 300°F (150°C) on a candy thermometer, about 15 minutes.

Remove pan from heat and carefully stir in butter and baking soda (mixture will foam up). Remove baking sheet from oven and pour in brittle mixture. Use the back of a greased spoon to spread out brittle as thinly as possible. Cool brittle completely.

Break into small pieces and store in an airtight container at room temperature.

DEVILED
EGGS

This **'70s classic** has staying power and for good reason. It's the come-from-behind hit at any gathering!

Classic Deviled Eggs

Makes 12 halves

....

6 large eggs, at room temperature

¼ cup (60 mL) mayonnaise

1 tsp (5 mL) Dijon mustard

Hot sauce

Salt and pepper

2 tbsp (30 mL) finely chopped chives

Paprika

Maldon sea salt

....

Fill a medium saucepan with cold water and bring to a boil over high heat. Gently add eggs and cook for 10 minutes.

Remove eggs from pan and place in a bowl of ice water. When cool enough to handle, peel eggs and pat dry with paper towels.

Halve eggs lengthwise and spoon yolks into a small bowl. Add mayonnaise and mustard and stir until smooth. Season to taste with hot sauce, salt, and pepper. Fill egg whites with yolk mixture, arrange on a platter, and garnish with a sprinkling of chives, paprika, and Maldon sea salt. Serve immediately.

Curried Deviled Eggs

Makes 12 halves

....

1 tsp (5 mL) Madras-style curry powder

6 hard-boiled eggs, halved lengthwise

¼ cup (60 mL) mayonnaise

2 tsp (10 mL) honey

Hot sauce

Salt and pepper

2 tbsp (30 mL) very finely diced Gala apple

Maldon sea salt and cracked black pepper

....

In a small skillet over medium-high heat, dry-toast curry powder, stirring constantly, until fragrant, about 1 minute, then pour in a small bowl. Add egg yolks, mayonnaise, and honey and stir until smooth. Season to taste with hot sauce, salt, and pepper. Fill egg whites with yolk mixture, arrange on a platter, and garnish with a sprinkling of apple, Maldon sea salt, and cracked pepper. Serve immediately.

Crab Deviled Eggs

Makes 12 halves

·········

6 hard-boiled eggs, halved lengthwise

¼ cup (60 mL) cooked crabmeat, picked through

¼ cup (60 mL) mayonnaise

1 tsp (5 mL) Dijon mustard

1 tsp (5 mL) sherry vinegar

½ tsp (2 mL) Worcestershire sauce

Hot sauce

Lemon juice

Salt and pepper

Old Bay Seasoning (page 169 or store-bought)

·········

In a small bowl, combine egg yolks, crabmeat, mayonnaise, mustard, vinegar, and Worcestershire sauce; stir until smooth. Season to taste with hot sauce, lemon juice, salt, and pepper. Fill egg whites with yolk mixture, arrange on a platter, and garnish with a sprinkling of Old Bay Seasoning. Serve immediately.

Bacon & Smoked Paprika Deviled Eggs

Makes 12 halves

·········

6 hard-boiled eggs, halved lengthwise

¼ cup (60 mL) mayonnaise

2 slices bacon, cooked and finely chopped

1 tbsp (15 mL) finely chopped parsley

Hot sauce

Salt and pepper

2 green onions, thinly sliced

Smoked paprika

Maldon sea salt

·········

In a small bowl, combine egg yolks, mayonnaise, bacon, and parsley; stir until smooth. Season to taste with hot sauce, salt, and pepper. Fill egg whites with yolk mixture, arrange on a platter, and garnish with a sprinkling of green onions, paprika, and Maldon sea salt. Serve immediately.

Chips & Caramelized Onion Dip

....

I love chips and dip. I really do. In this recipe, the caramelized onion flavor is fantastic with the crisp, salty fried potato chips. *Serves 4*

....

Caramelized Onion Dip

2 onions, halved and thinly sliced
1 tbsp (15 mL) olive oil
2 cups (500 mL) sour cream
1 tbsp (15 mL) finely chopped chives
1 tbsp (15 mL) finely chopped parsley
Grated zest of 1 lemon
Salt and pepper

Yukon Gold Potato Chips

3 cups (750 mL) vegetable oil
2 Yukon Gold Potatoes, scrubbed, patted dry, and thinly sliced with a mandoline
2 tsp (10 mL) chopped rosemary
Salt and pepper

....

For the onion dip, in a medium skillet over medium heat, combine oil and onions. Cook, stirring occasionally, until onions are caramelized, about 20 minutes. Remove pan from heat and let onions cool to room temperature.

In a medium bowl, stir together sour cream, chives, parsley, and lemon zest; season to taste with salt and pepper. Stir in cooled onions, cover, and refrigerate for at least 2 hours before serving.

For the Yukon Gold potato chips, in a medium, deep saucepan, heat oil to 325°F (160°C). Working in batches, add potato slices to hot oil and fry until crisp and golden, about 3 minutes. Use a slotted spoon to transfer chips to a paper-towel-lined plate to drain. While still hot, sprinkle each batch of chips with rosemary, salt, and pepper.

Steak Tartare

How many favorites can I have? Lots! Tartare sounds fancy, tastes great, and is super-easy to prepare. There's no cooking! But you do want to be particular about the meat you use: high-quality fresh beef is crucial. Hand-chop the meat just before serving. Serve with crusty bread, potato chips (page 245), or crispy fried wontons. *Serves 4*

1 lb (450 g) beef tenderloin, cut in ¼-inch (5 mm) dice
⅓ cup (75 mL) finely chopped Vidalia onion
3 tbsp (45 mL) finely diced cornichons
2 tbsp (30 mL) small capers, finely chopped
1 large anchovy, minced
1 clove garlic, minced
2 tbsp (30 mL) finely chopped parsley
2 tbsp (30 mL) finely chopped chives
2 tbsp (30 mL) mayonnaise
1 tbsp (15 mL) extra-virgin olive oil
1 tbsp (15 mL) ketchup
1 tbsp (15 mL) Dijon mustard
1 tsp (5 mL) Worcestershire sauce
½ tsp (2 mL) hot sauce
Kosher salt and cracked black pepper
1 baguette, sliced and toasted

In a large bowl, combine beef, onions, cornichons, capers, anchovy, and garlic. Stir to mix, cover, and refrigerate for at least 20 minutes.

Meanwhile, in a small bowl, combine parsley, chives, mayonnaise, oil, ketchup, mustard, Worcestershire sauce, and hot sauce. Stir until well combined, then stir into chilled beef mixture. Season to taste with salt and pepper. Serve immediately with toasted baguette slices.

Meatballs with Tomato Basil Sauce

These rank as one of my favorite snacks. I just love meatballs. I think everyone does. Ricotta cheese makes these extra-moist, and they are kept light with the tomato basil sauce. Make more than you need and eat the rest with pasta the following night. *Makes about 36 small meatballs*

Tomato Basil Sauce

Makes about 3½ cups (875 mL)

3 tbsp (45 mL) olive oil

1 small onion, finely chopped

3 large cloves garlic, minced

1 can (28 oz/796 mL) diced tomatoes

2 sprigs basil

1 tsp (5 mL) granulated sugar

Salt and pepper

½ lb (225 g) lean ground beef

½ lb (225 g) spicy Italian sausage, casings removed

2 eggs, beaten

2 cloves garlic, minced

1 lb (450 g) ricotta cheese, drained

1 cup (250 mL) fresh bread torn in small pieces,
  soaked in milk, squeezed dry

½ cup (125 mL) finely chopped onion

¼ cup (60 mL) grated Parmesan cheese,
  plus more for garnish

1 tsp (5 mL) red pepper flakes

Salt and pepper

All-purpose flour, for dusting

Olive oil, for frying

2 cups (500 mL) Tomato Basil Sauce

2 tbsp (30 mL) finely chopped parsley

For the tomato basil sauce, in a large skillet over medium heat, combine oil, onions, and garlic. Cook, stirring frequently, until onions are soft, about 5 minutes. Stir in tomatoes, basil, and sugar. Bring sauce to a boil, reduce heat to low, and cook, stirring occasionally, until sauce thickens, about 30 minutes.

Remove sauce from heat and season with salt and pepper. Remove basil sprigs if you like.

In a large bowl, combine beef, sausage meat, eggs, garlic, ricotta, bread, onions, ¼ cup (60 mL) Parmesan, red pepper flakes, and salt and pepper. Mix until well combined, then cover and refrigerate for at least 2 hours.

Preheat oven to 300°F (150°C).

Sprinkle a generous amount of flour on a baking sheet. With floured hands, gently shape chilled meat mixture into walnut-sized balls. Place on floured tray.

In a large skillet, heat about ¾ inch (2 cm) of oil over medium-high heat until slightly smoking. Working in batches, gently place meatballs into hot oil and fry, turning just once, until golden brown, about 3 minutes per side. Transfer to a clean baking sheet and keep warm in the oven while frying the rest.

Spoon warmed tomato sauce onto a platter, arrange meatballs on top, and garnish with parsley and a sprinkling of Parmesan. Serve immediately.

Shrimp with Prosciutto, Lemon & Chili

....

Shrimp are deliciously meaty. This recipe uses prosciutto to lend some saltiness and a good squeeze of lemon to perk them up. Jumbo shrimp give you the juiciest bite, but any size will do. *Serves 4*

....

¼ cup (60 mL) unsalted butter, softened

2 cloves garlic, minced

2 green onions, chopped

Juice of ½ lemon

2 tbsp (30 mL) chopped parsley

½ tsp (2 mL) red pepper flakes

2 tbsp (30 mL) olive oil

4 slices prosciutto

1 lb (450 g) raw shrimp (size 21/25), peeled and deveined

Salt and pepper

Lemon wedges, for garnish

....

In a food processor, combine butter, garlic, green onions, lemon juice, parsley, and red pepper flakes; pulse to combine. Set aside.

In a large skillet over medium-high heat, add oil and prosciutto. Fry prosciutto until crispy, about 2 minutes per side, then transfer to paper towels to drain.

Add shrimp to oil in skillet and sauté, turning once, until pink and firm, about 2 minutes per side. Add reserved butter mixture, toss to coat, and season to taste with salt and pepper.

Transfer shrimp to a platter, garnish with prosciutto and lemon wedges, and serve immediately.

Baked Brie with Fruit & Nut Honey

....

I always have lemon thyme honey on hand ready to go. I keep it in mason jars and put it on everything: with yogurt for breakfast, with ice cream for dessert, and in this case, with baked Brie for an awesome sweet and sticky snack. Be sure to pile on the dried fruits and nuts. It looks great. *Serves 4*

....

1 wheel Brie (about 8 oz/225 g)
1 cup (250 mL) assorted dried fruits and nuts
1 cup (250 mL) Lemon Thyme Honey (page 13)
½ tsp (2 mL) black pepper
Baguette slices

....

Preheat oven to 350°F (180°C).

Place Brie in an ovenproof dish and bake for 15 minutes.

Meanwhile, in a small saucepan, combine fruits and nuts, honey, and black pepper. Heat over medium-low heat until warmed through, about 10 minutes.

Top Brie with honey mixture and serve immediately with sliced baguette.

Cauliflower Tempura with Lemon Rosemary Sour Cream

This tempura is really light and makes for easy eating. Rosemary features heavily here, in the batter and the dip. It's so aromatic and adds a lot of character to the sour cream dipping sauce. *Serves 4*

Lemon Rosemary Sour Cream

¾ cup (175 mL) sour cream

1 tsp (5 mL) grated lemon zest

1 tbsp (15 mL) lemon juice

1 tsp (5 mL) finely chopped rosemary

1 clove garlic, minced

Cauliflower Tempura

1 cup (250 mL) all-purpose flour

¼ cup (60 mL) cornstarch

1 tsp (5 mL) baking powder

1 tsp (5 mL) salt, plus more for garnish

1 tsp (5 mL) chopped rosemary

¼ tsp (1 mL) smoked paprika

1¼ cups (300 mL) club soda

Vegetable oil, for deep-frying

3 cups (750 mL) cauliflower florets

For the lemon rosemary sour cream, in a small bowl, stir together sour cream, lemon zest and juice, rosemary, and garlic. Cover and refrigerate until ready to serve.

For the cauliflower tempura, in a medium bowl, whisk together flour, cornstarch, baking powder, 1 tsp (5 mL) salt, rosemary, and paprika. Whisk in club soda just until combined.

In a medium, deep saucepan over medium heat, heat 4 inches (10 cm) of oil to 365°F (185°C).

Working in batches, dip cauliflower florets in batter, letting excess drip back into bowl, and place gently in oil. Cook until golden, about 3 minutes. Transfer florets to paper towels and sprinkle lightly with salt.

Serve cauliflower tempura immediately with dipping sauce.

Parmesan Truffled Popcorn

I remember when popcorn flavorings were first at cinema concession stands. This is an easy way to jazz up your bowl of popcorn when it's movie night at home. Make lots … it goes fast! *Makes about 8 cups (2 L)*

3 tbsp (45 mL) vegetable oil
⅓ cup (75 mL) popping corn kernels
1 tbsp (15 mL) grated Parmesan cheese
2 tsp (10 mL) chopped chives
1 tsp (5 mL) truffle oil
Salt and pepper

In a large saucepan with a tight-fitting lid, heat vegetable oil over high heat. Add kernels in a single layer, cover, and cook, shaking pot constantly until sound of popping slows to several seconds between pops.

Pour popcorn into a large bowl. Sprinkle with Parmesan and chives, drizzle with truffle oil, season to taste with salt and pepper, and toss well to combine. Serve immediately.

Chickpea Hummus

Jazz up this classic with some roasted peppers, toasted pine nuts, pesto, or hot sauce right on top. Serve with warm grilled flatbreads.

Makes 2 cups (500 mL)

1 can (19 oz/540 mL) chickpeas, drained and rinsed
2 large cloves garlic, coarsely chopped
¼ cup (60 mL) tahini
Juice of 1 lemon
¼ cup (60 mL) olive oil
Salt and pepper

Place chickpeas and garlic in a food processor and pulse into a coarse paste. With motor running, drizzle in tahini, lemon juice, and oil; process until smooth.

Spoon hummus into a serving bowl, season to taste with salt and pepper, and serve immediately.

Parmesan Shortbread

....

These are perfect served alongside a beautiful cheese board. Better than those goldfish any day! *Makes about 24 shortbreads*

....

½ cup (125 mL) all-purpose flour
½ cup (125 mL) unsalted butter, cut in ½-inch (1 cm) cubes
1 cup (250 mL) grated Parmesan cheese
¼ cup (60 mL) whole (3.25%) milk
1 tbsp (15 mL) cracked black pepper

....

In a food processor, combine flour and butter; pulse until mixture resembles coarse meal. Add Parmesan and milk; pulse until mixture forms a ball.

Transfer dough to a piece of plastic wrap and shape into a log 1 inch (2.5 cm) wide. Roll up log and twist ends of plastic closed. Refrigerate for 1 hour.

Preheat oven to 350°F (180°C).

Cut dough into ¼-inch (5 mm) rounds, arrange on a baking sheet, and sprinkle tops with cracked black pepper.

Bake shortbreads until golden brown, about 10 minutes. Transfer to racks and let cool to room temperature before serving.

Jalapeño Poppers

Sometimes there are cravings, and this bar-worthy appetizer can be one of them. In this recipe, the jalapeños' heat is tamed with the Boursin cheese, a herbed cream cheese that I always keep on hand. These are as easy to make as they are to pop in your mouth. *Makes 24 poppers*

Popper Filling

¼ cup (60 mL) Boursin cheese

¼ cup (60 mL) shredded Cheddar cheese

¼ cup (60 mL) heavy (35%) cream

2 tsp (10 mL) Dijon mustard

½ tsp (2 mL) ground cumin

½ tsp (2 mL) ground coriander

¼ tsp (1 mL) cayenne pepper

¼ tsp (1 mL) smoked paprika

Salt and pepper

24 jalapeño peppers

Tempura Batter

½ cup (125 mL) all-purpose flour

2 tbsp (30 mL) cornstarch

½ tsp (2 mL) baking powder

½ cup (125 mL) club soda

2 cups (500 mL) vegetable oil

Salt and pepper

For the popper filling, in a food processor, combine Boursin, Cheddar, cream, mustard, cumin, coriander, cayenne, and paprika; process until smooth. Season to taste with salt and pepper, then spoon into a piping bag fitted with a small plain tip.

Slit jalapeños open lengthwise and scrape out seeds and ribs. Pipe filling mixture into cavities. Refrigerate for at least 1 hour.

For the tempura batter and poppers, in a medium bowl, whisk together flour, cornstarch, and baking powder. Whisk in club soda to form a batter.

In a medium, deep saucepan, heat oil over medium heat to 375°F (190°C). Working in batches, dip stuffed jalapeños in batter and deep-fry in oil until golden, about 4 minutes. Transfer to paper towels to drain and season to taste with salt and pepper. Let jalapeño poppers cool for 5 minutes before serving.

SWEET DREAMS

Vanilla Flan

Don't let the name fool you—this classic dessert is simple and delicious! This restaurant staple should be enjoyed at home, and often. *Serves 4*

Caramel

½ cup (125 mL) granulated sugar

2 tbsp (30 mL) water

Flan

2 cups (500 mL) heavy (35%) cream

1 tsp (5 mL) vanilla extract

Pinch of salt

½ cup (125 mL) granulated sugar

5 large egg yolks

Preheat oven to 325°F (160°C).

For the caramel, in a small saucepan, combine sugar and water. Stir over medium heat until sugar has dissolved, then increase heat to medium-high and bring mixture to a boil. Cook, swirling pot occasionally but not stirring, until caramel is amber in color, about 6 minutes. Working quickly, divide among four 1-cup (250 mL) ramekins, swirling to evenly coat bottoms with caramel. Set aside to harden.

For the flan, in a medium saucepan over medium-high heat, bring cream, vanilla, and salt to a simmer.

Meanwhile, in a large bowl, whisk together sugar and egg yolks until sugar has completely dissolved. Gradually whisk in warm cream mixture until well combined. Strain custard through a fine-mesh sieve into a medium pitcher and let stand for 5 minutes to eliminate bubbles.

Place ramekins in a roasting pan and fill almost to the top with custard. Place pan in oven, pour in enough boiling water to reach halfway up sides of ramekins, and cover pan with foil. Bake custards until set but still slightly jiggly in the center, about 25 minutes.

Transfer ramekins to a rack and let cool to room temperature. Cover with plastic wrap and refrigerate overnight.

To serve, run the point of a small knife around edge of each custard to loosen, turn ramekin over onto a plate, shake gently, then slowly lift so that caramel will run down over flan. Serve immediately.

Banana Fritters with Toasted Coconut & Honey

....

I love these fritters. Their super-light coconut batter makes them the perfect summertime treat. *Serves 4*

....

½ cup (125 mL) all-purpose flour

2 tbsp (30 mL) cornstarch

½ tsp (2 mL) baking powder

½ tsp (2 mL) salt

½ cup (125 mL) ginger ale

¾ cup (175 mL) sweetened shredded coconut, lightly toasted

Vegetable oil, for deep-frying

4 ripe bananas, peeled, halved lengthwise, and cut in 3-inch (8 cm) pieces

¼ cup (60 mL) honey

....

In a medium bowl, whisk together flour, cornstarch, baking powder, and salt. Add ginger ale and ½ cup (125 mL) toasted coconut and whisk until a crêpe-like batter forms.

In a medium, deep saucepan over medium-high heat, heat 4 inches (10 cm) of oil to 375°F (190°C).

Working in batches, dip banana pieces into batter, gently place in hot oil, and fry until golden, about 4 minutes. Transfer fritters to paper towels to drain.

Place warm fritters on a platter, drizzle with honey, and sprinkle with remaining coconut. Serve immediately.

Stuffed Baked Apples with Caramel Sauce

When filming *Pitchin' In* in Nova Scotia's Annapolis Valley, I used tart Gravenstein apples to make this absolutely scrumptious apples-in-baked-apples dessert. *Serves 4*

Caramel Sauce

1 cup (250 mL) granulated sugar

¼ cup (60 mL) water

Pinch of salt

2 tbsp (30 mL) unsalted butter

2 tbsp (30 mL) heavy (35%) cream

Baked Apples

2 tbsp (30 mL) packed brown sugar

2 tbsp (30 mL) unsalted butter

½ cup (125 mL) finely diced apple

1 cup (250 mL) all-purpose flour

¼ cup (60 mL) granulated sugar

Pinch of salt

¼ cup (60 mL) whole (3.25%) milk

¼ cup (60 mL) unsalted butter, melted

1 tsp (5 mL) vanilla extract

4 large baking apples, such as Gravenstein, Cortland, Honeycrisp, or Northern Spy

For the caramel sauce, in a small saucepan, stir together sugar, water, and salt. Bring to a boil over medium-high heat and cook, without stirring or shaking pot, until water has evaporated and sugar is light golden brown, about 8 minutes. Remove pot from heat and whisk in butter and cream until smooth. Keep sauce warm until ready to serve.

Preheat oven to 350°F (180°C).

For the baked apples, in a small skillet over medium heat, stir together brown sugar and 2 tbsp (30 mL) butter until smooth. Add diced apples and cook, stirring frequently, until fork-tender, about 5 minutes. Remove from heat.

In a medium bowl, whisk together flour, sugar, and salt.

In a small bowl, whisk together milk, melted butter, and vanilla. Stir into flour mixture to form a batter. Add cooked apple mixture and stir until well combined. Set aside.

Slice off top third of each apple. Using a teaspoon or melon baller, carefully scoop out core and flesh to within ¼ inch (5 mm) of bottom and sides.

Spoon batter into apples. Place apples in a small baking dish and bake until fork-tender, about 40 minutes.

Serve apples warm with a generous amount of caramel sauce spooned over top.

Blueberry Buckle

....

This buckle is fully loaded. The beautiful blueberries and crisp streusel topping make this an all-day cake. *Serves 12*

....

Streusel Topping

1 cup (250 mL) all-purpose flour

½ cup (125 mL) packed brown sugar

¼ tsp (1 mL) salt

½ cup (125 mL) cold unsalted butter,
    cut in pieces

Cake

2 cups (500 mL) all-purpose flour

1½ tsp (7 mL) baking powder

½ tsp (2 mL) salt

½ cup (125 mL) unsalted butter,
    at room temperature

¾ cup (175 mL) granulated sugar

1 large egg

1 tsp (5 mL) vanilla extract

½ cup (125 mL) milk

5 cups (1.25 L) fresh blueberries

....

Preheat oven to 350°F (180°C). Grease and flour a 10-inch (3 L) springform pan.

For the streusel topping, in a small bowl, combine flour, sugar, salt, and butter. Using a fork, mash together until crumbly. Set aside.

For the cake, in a medium bowl, sift together flour, baking powder, and salt.

In the bowl of a stand mixer fitted with the paddle attachment, cream together butter and sugar on medium speed until light and fluffy, about 3 minutes. Reduce speed to low and beat in egg and vanilla.

Beat in half the flour mixture, then the milk, and then remaining flour mixture. Gently fold in blueberries.

Spread batter in prepared pan and top with reserved streusel mixture. Bake until a toothpick inserted in the center of cake comes out clean, about 60 minutes.

Transfer cake to a rack and cool for 10 minutes before removing sides of pan, then let cake cool for another 15 minutes before serving.

Grape Almond Clafoutis

. . . .

My clafoutis riffs on the original French recipe, substituting perfect sweet grapes for the traditional cherries. But cherries are good too!

Serves 4

. . . .

1 tbsp (15 mL) unsalted butter, softened

6 large eggs

1¼ cups (300 mL) whole (3.25%) milk

6 tbsp (90 mL) granulated sugar

2 tbsp (30 mL) amaretto

1 tbsp (15 mL) vanilla extract

Pinch of salt

¾ cup (175 mL) all-purpose flour, sifted

3 cups (750 mL) seedless red grapes

½ cup (125 mL) blanched sliced almonds

Icing sugar, for dusting

. . . .

Preheat oven to 400°F (200°C). Grease four 1-cup (250 mL) baking dishes with the butter. Place on a parchment-lined baking sheet.

In a large bowl, whisk eggs. Add milk, sugar, amaretto, vanilla, and salt and whisk until well combined. Add flour and whisk until smooth. Stir in grapes.

Spoon batter into baking dishes and sprinkle almonds over top. Bake until a skewer inserted in center comes out clean, about 30 minutes.

Let clafoutis cool for 5 minutes. Dust with icing sugar and serve immediately.

Sweet Lime Squares

....

I adore limes. Lime juice and lime zest, and I'm smiling! These attractive little squares are great go-to sweets. *Makes 16 squares*

....

Crust

1⅔ cups (400 mL) graham cracker crumbs (5 oz/140 g)
3 tbsp (45 mL) packed brown sugar
Pinch of salt
4 tbsp (60 mL) unsalted butter, melted

Filling

2 oz (55 g) cream cheese, softened
1 tbsp (15 mL) grated lime zest
Pinch of salt
1 can (14 oz/398 mL) sweetened condensed milk
1 egg yolk
½ cup (125 mL) lime juice

....

Preheat oven to 325°F (160°C). Line an 8-inch ((2 L) square cake pan with foil and generously grease foil.

For the crust, in a food processor, combine graham crackers crumbs, sugar, and salt. Pulse until combined. Drizzle butter over crumb mixture and pulse until crumbs are moistened.

Press crumbs firmly into bottom of prepared pan. Bake until golden brown, about 20 minutes. Transfer pan to a rack to cool.

For the filling, in a medium bowl, combine cream cheese, lime zest, salt, and condensed milk; whisk vigorously until smooth. Whisk in egg yolk and lime juice until combined.

Pour filling into cooled crust, spread to corners, and smooth top with a spatula. Bake until filling begins to slightly pull away from sides of pan, about 20 minutes.

Transfer pan to a rack and let cool to room temperature. Refrigerate until chilled. Cut into 16 squares.

Lemon Cake

This classic cake is as elegant as it is delicious. The olive oil makes for an extra-moist mouthful, balanced with the zesty lemon drizzle.

Serves 10

Lemon Syrup

¼ cup (60 mL) granulated sugar
¼ cup (60 mL) water
1 lemon, thinly sliced

Lemon Cake

1⅔ cups (400 mL) all-purpose flour
1½ tsp (7 mL) baking powder
Pinch of salt
6 tbsp (90 mL) unsalted butter, melted
⅓ cup (75 mL) olive oil
2 tbsp (30 mL) lemon juice
¾ cup (175 mL) granulated sugar
Grated zest of 2 lemons
4 large eggs, at room temperature
3 tbsp (45 mL) whole (3.25%) milk

For the lemon syrup, in a small saucepan, combine sugar, water, and lemon slices. Bring to a boil over medium heat, stirring occasionally. When sugar has completely dissolved, remove pan from heat and let mixture cool to room temperature.

For the lemon cake, preheat oven to 375°F (190°C). Grease a 9-inch (2.5 L) springform pan.

In a medium bowl, whisk together flour, baking powder, and salt.

In a small bowl, whisk together melted butter, olive oil, and lemon juice.

In the bowl of a stand mixer fitted with the whisk attachment, combine sugar, lemon zest, and eggs. Whisk on medium-high speed until mixture is pale yellow, about 5 minutes. Add milk and whisk to combine.

Add flour mixture and whisk on low speed until moistened. Slowly whisk in butter mixture until well combined.

Pour batter into prepared pan. Bake until a toothpick inserted in center of cake comes out clean, about 30 minutes.

Transfer cake to a rack and let cool for 10 minutes before removing sides of pan. Place cake on a serving plate, arrange glazed lemon slices on top, and drizzle with lemon syrup.

Hazelnut Pear Tart

·········

The perfect dessert! This tart is an awesome centerpiece. Serve to anyone, anytime. *Serves 10*

·········

Pastry

1⅓ cups (325 mL) all-purpose flour

½ cup (125 mL) granulated sugar

½ cup (125 mL) cold unsalted butter, cut in ½-inch (1 cm) cubes

1 large egg

Hazelnut Filling

⅔ cup (150 mL) whole blanched roasted hazelnuts

¼ cup (60 mL) granulated sugar

⅓ cup (75 mL) all-purpose flour

4 tbsp (60 mL) butter, at room temperature

2 large eggs

Pear Layer

3 large pears, halved lengthwise, cored, and thinly sliced

⅓ cup (75 mL) granulated sugar

½ tsp (2 mL) cinnamon

·········

For the pastry, in a food processor, combine all ingredients and pulse until dough cleans sides of bowl. Wrap dough in plastic wrap and refrigerate for 30 minutes.

For the hazelnut filling, in the cleaned food processor, pulse hazelnuts with sugar until finely ground. Add flour, butter, and eggs; process until mixture is a paste-like consistency. Set aside.

For the pear layer, in a large bowl, toss pears with sugar and cinnamon. Set aside.

Preheat oven to 375°F (190°C). Butter a 9-inch (23 cm) tart pan with removable bottom.

To assemble tart, on a floured work surface, roll out chilled dough to ⅛-inch (3 mm) thickness. Press into bottom and up sides of prepared pan. Trim edges.

Spread hazelnut mixture over bottom of pastry. Fan pear slices in an attractive overlapping pattern on top.

Bake tart until golden, about 40 minutes. Let cool to room temperature before serving.

Cheesecake in a Jar

A perfect no-bake cheesecake recipe that will have everyone asking for seconds! *Makes 6 jars*

1¼ cups (300 mL) graham cracker crumbs

4 tbsp (60 mL) butter, melted

¼ cup (60 mL) packed brown sugar

1 cup (250 mL) heavy (35%) cream

4 oz (115 g) cream cheese, at room temperature

½ cup (125 mL) icing sugar

1 cup (250 mL) strawberry jam

Preheat oven to 350°F (180°C).

In a small bowl, stir together graham crumbs, melted butter, and brown sugar until well combined. Evenly divide mixture among six 1-cup (250 mL) mason jars, gently pressing down to pack crumbs on the bottom.

Place jars on a baking sheet and bake until crumbs are set, about 5 minutes. Let cool.

Meanwhile, in a large bowl, whisk cream to soft peaks.

In the bowl of a stand mixer fitted with the paddle attachment, beat cream cheese with icing sugar until smooth. Fold in whipped cream until well combined. Spoon mixture into jars.

Top each cheesecake with strawberry jam, then refrigerate until ready to serve.

Sweet Potato Bourbon Cake

This recipe is simple and flexible. Switch out the sweet potato for pumpkin purée, the bourbon for your favorite easy-drinking alternative.

....

3 cups (750 mL) unbleached all-purpose flour

2 tsp (10 mL) baking powder

2 tsp (10 mL) cinnamon

2 tsp (10 mL) ground ginger

1 tsp (5 mL) salt

1 tsp (5 mL) baking soda

½ tsp (2 mL) nutmeg

⅛ tsp (0.5 mL) ground cloves

¼ cup (60 mL) unsalted butter, softened

½ cup (125 mL) vegetable oil

4 large eggs

2½ cups (625 mL) packed dark brown sugar

2 cups (500 mL) puréed cooked sweet potato

¾ cup (175 mL) buttermilk

3 tbsp (45 mL) bourbon

1½ tsp (7 mL) vanilla extract

1 cup (250 mL) chopped walnuts, toasted

Whipped cream for serving

Bourbon Glaze

¾ cup (175 mL) packed dark brown sugar

½ cup (125 mL) unsalted butter

2 tbsp (30 mL) corn syrup

4 tsp (20 mL) bourbon

⅛ tsp (0.5 mL) salt

⅓ cup (75 mL) heavy (35%) cream

1¼ cups (300 mL) icing sugar, sifted

1 tsp (5 mL) vanilla extract

Preheat oven to 350°F (180°C). Generously grease and flour a 10-cup (2.5 L) tube pan.

In a large bowl, sift together flour, baking powder, cinnamon, ginger, salt, baking soda, nutmeg, and cloves. Set aside.

In the bowl of a stand mixer fitted with the paddle attachment, beat butter on medium speed until creamy. Slowly beat in oil. Increase speed to high and beat in eggs one at a time. Add brown sugar and beat until mixture is light and fluffy, about 4 minutes, scraping down the sides of the bowl as needed.

Reduce speed to medium-low and beat in sweet potato. Reduce speed to low and slowly beat in buttermilk, bourbon, and vanilla. Gradually add flour mixture, mixing just until combined, then fold in walnuts.

Spoon batter into prepared pan and tap pan on work surface to settle batter. Bake until a toothpick inserted in center of cake comes out clean, about 60 minutes. Transfer cake to a rack and let cool for 15 minutes.

While cake cools, make the glaze. In a medium saucepan, stir together brown sugar, butter, corn syrup, bourbon, and salt. Cook over medium heat, stirring frequently, until butter melts and sugar has dissolved, about 2 minutes.

Increase heat to high, add cream, and bring to a boil. Boil for 1 minute, stirring occasionally, then remove from heat. Add icing sugar and vanilla and whisk until glaze is smooth. Let cool for 5 minutes before glazing cake.

Remove cake from pan. Pour glaze evenly over cake. Let sit for 15 minutes to allow glaze to harden slightly. Serve cake slices with a dollop of whipped cream.

Blondies

I like serving blondies and brownies together—the mixed colors look so inviting. But, let's be honest, I'm lucky if they make it out of the pan. *Makes 12 squares*

· · · · · · · · ·

2 cups (500 mL) all-purpose flour

1½ tsp (7 mL) baking powder

¼ tsp (1 mL) salt

1¼ cups (300 mL) packed brown sugar

½ cup (125 mL) granulated sugar

1 tsp (5 mL) vanilla extract

2 large eggs

¾ cup (175 mL) unsalted butter, melted

2 cups (500 mL) white chocolate chips

· · · · · · · · ·

Preheat oven to 350°F (180°C). Grease and flour a 13- × 9-inch (3 L) cake pan.

In a large bowl, whisk together flour, baking powder, and salt.

In another large bowl, whisk together brown sugar, granulated sugar, vanilla, and eggs until smooth. Add butter and whisk to combine.

Stir in flour mixture just until combined, then fold in white chocolate chips.

Spread batter in prepared pan and bake until a toothpick inserted in center comes out clean, about 20 minutes. Let blondies cool completely before cutting into squares.

Brownies

•••••••••

These brownies are one of my favorite treats to eat—chocolatey rich, quick, and easy to make! *Makes 12 squares*

•••••••••

12 oz (340 g) dark chocolate, chopped
1¼ cups (300 mL) unsalted butter
1¼ cups (300 mL) all-purpose flour
⅓ cup (75 mL) cocoa powder
½ tsp (2 mL) salt
2½ cups (625 mL) granulated sugar
5 large eggs
4 tsp (20 mL) vanilla extract
1 cup (250 mL) milk chocolate chips

•••••••••

Preheat oven to 350°F (180°C). Grease and flour a 13- × 9-inch (3 L) cake pan.

In a medium heatproof bowl set over a small pot of simmering water, melt dark chocolate and butter, stirring occasionally. Remove from heat and let cool.

In a medium bowl, whisk together flour, cocoa powder, and salt.

In a large bowl, whisk together sugar, eggs, and vanilla until sugar has completely dissolved. Stir in cooled chocolate mixture until well combined. Stir in flour mixture until combined, then fold in chocolate chips.

Spoon batter into prepared pan and bake until a toothpick inserted in the center comes out clean, about 25 minutes. Let brownies cool completely before cutting into squares.

Butterscotch Pudding

This dessert is an immediate hit. Our
Kathleen, the talented photographer for this
beautiful book, was barely able to get the
shot! It's easy to make and even easier to eat.

Serves 4

....

1½ cups (375 mL) heavy (35%) cream

½ cup (125 mL) whole (3.25%) milk

½ cup (125 mL) granulated sugar

½ cup (125 mL) water

5 egg yolks

....

Preheat oven to 350°F (180°C).

In a medium saucepan over low heat, bring cream and milk to a simmer.

In another medium saucepan, stir together sugar and water. Bring to a boil over medium-high heat, then reduce heat to medium and cook, without stirring, until sugar has dissolved and turns golden brown, about 15 minutes.

Slowly whisk warm cream mixture into caramel until well combined.

In a medium bowl, whisk egg yolks. Whisking constantly, very slowly ladle a little caramel mixture into egg yolks to temper eggs, then slowly whisk yolk mixture into caramel mixture until well combined.

Ladle pudding mixture into four ½-cup (125 mL) ramekins. Place ramekins in a baking dish or small roasting pan and add enough boiling water to come halfway up sides of ramekins.

Bake puddings until just set, about 30 minutes. Transfer ramekins to a rack and let cool to room temperature. Cover and refrigerate overnight.

Chocolate Peanut Butter Mousse

Peanut butter and chocolate—the great equalizer, loved by kids and adults alike. This classic combination is perfect in this fun and decadent dessert. *Serves 4*

1⅔ cups (400 mL) heavy (35%) cream

2 tsp (10 mL) vanilla extract

½ tsp (2 mL) salt

4 egg whites, at room temperature

½ cup (125 mL) granulated sugar

¾ cup (175 mL) chopped bittersweet chocolate, melted and cooled slightly

½ cup (125 mL) smooth peanut butter, melted and cooled

Chopped salted peanuts, for garnish

In a large bowl, beat cream, vanilla, and salt until stiff peaks form.

In another large bowl, beat egg whites until soft peaks form. Slowly beat in sugar and continue beating until stiff, shiny peaks form. Gently fold in chocolate and peanut butter. Gently but thoroughly fold in whipped cream.

Spoon into 4 dessert dishes, garnish with peanuts, and refrigerate until ready to serve.

Chocolate Tart with Salted Caramel Sauce

....

This dessert is so popular at Ruby Watchco that we have to make extras for diners (and staff!) to take away. It's impossible to resist the salted caramel sauce. Trust me, I know from experience! *Serves 8*

....

Sweet Pastry Shell

1½ cups (375 mL) all-purpose flour

½ cup (125 mL) icing sugar

¼ tsp (1 mL) salt

4½ oz (130 g) cold unsalted butter, cut in small pieces

1 egg, lightly beaten

Chocolate Filling

1¼ cups (300 mL) heavy (35%) cream

1¼ cups (300 mL) finely chopped bittersweet chocolate

2 egg yolks, beaten

1 tsp (5 mL) vanilla extract

¼ tsp (1 mL) salt

....

For the sweet pastry shell, in a food processor, combine flour, sugar, salt, and butter. Pulse until mixture resembles coarse meal. Add egg and continue pulsing until the dough starts to form clumps.

Turn dough out onto a work surface and knead until just combined. Wrap in plastic wrap and refrigerate for 1 hour.

Preheat oven to 400°F (200°C).

On a lightly floured work surface, roll out dough into an 11-inch (28 cm) circle. Carefully fit it into a 9-inch (23 cm) tart pan with removable bottom. Pat some of the overhanging dough back in around the edge to make the sides of the tart shell thicker than the bottom. Trim excess pastry from edges. Refrigerate tart shell until firm, about 30 minutes.

With a fork, prick bottom of chilled pastry tart at ½-inch (1 cm) intervals. Line with parchment paper and fill with pie weights or dried beans.

Bake pastry shell until the rim starts to turn golden, about 15 minutes. Remove weights and parchment, return shell to oven, and bake until golden, about 10 minutes more. Transfer shell to a rack and let cool to room temperature. Reduce oven temperature to 350°F (180°C).

Make the filling while the tart shell cools. In a medium saucepan over medium heat, bring cream to a gentle boil. Add chocolate and stir until melted.

Remove pan from heat and whisk a little chocolate mixture into egg yolks, then whisk egg mixture into chocolate mixture along with vanilla and salt.

Spoon filling into tart shell and bake until set in the middle, about 30 minutes. Let tart cool completely before slicing and serving with caramel sauce (recipe follows).

Salted Caramel
Sauce

....

1 cup (250 mL) granulated sugar
¼ cup (60 mL) water
¼ tsp (1 mL) Maldon sea salt
2 tbsp (30 mL) unsalted butter
2 tbsp (30 mL) heavy (35%) cream

....

In a small saucepan, stir together sugar, water,
and salt. Bring to a boil over medium-high heat
and cook, without stirring or shaking pot, until
water has evaporated and sugar is light golden
brown, about 8 minutes.

Remove pot from heat and carefully
stir in butter and cream until smooth.
Keep sauce warm until ready
to serve.

Strawberry Icewine Float

Fresh strawberries signal to me that summer's sprung! In this recipe, they're double iced—mixed with an icewine and enjoyed over ice cream. *Serves 4*

1 cup (250 mL) finely diced strawberries
⅓ cup (75 mL) icewine
4 scoops strawberry ice cream
Champagne or sparkling water to cover

Stir together strawberries and icewine and let sit for half an hour.

Divide strawberries among 4 glasses. Top with a scoop of ice cream, add a splash of champagne, and serve immediately.

CHARLIE PICKLES & PORK CHOP'S FAVORITE TREAT

Charlie Pickles

Ninja Dog Treats

This one is for the dog lovers. My dogs Charlie Pickles and Pork Chop go crazy for these cookies, and yours will too! *Makes lots of ninjas*

1 lb (450 g) bacon, sliced crosswise in 1-inch (2.5 cm) pieces
13 oz (365 g) beef liver, cut in ½-inch (1 cm) pieces
¾ cup plus 1 tbsp (175 mL plus 15 mL) fine cornmeal
3 cups plus 3 tbsp (750 mL plus 45 mL) whole wheat flour
1 cup (250 mL) beef stock

Preheat oven to 350°F (180°C).

In a large nonstick skillet over medium heat, cook bacon, stirring occasionally, until golden brown, about 5 minutes. With a slotted spoon, transfer bacon to paper towels to drain.

Pour off all but 2 tbsp (30 mL) bacon fat from skillet, then add liver and cook, turning and smashing liver down with the back of a spoon, until broken down into a paste, about 5 minutes. Let cool slightly.

In a food processor, pulse bacon a few times. Add liver and cornmeal and process until you have a coarse mixture.

Transfer liver mixture to the bowl of a stand mixer fitted with the paddle attachment. Add flour and mix to combine. Slowly pour in stock and continue mixing until dough begins to gather around the paddle and feels moist to the touch.

Transfer dough to a work surface and knead until all flour is incorporated. Working in batches if necessary, place dough between two pieces of parchment paper and roll out to ⅜-inch (4 mm) thickness. Using ninja-shaped cookie cutters, stamp out dog treats and arrange ½ inch (1 cm) apart on parchment-lined baking sheets. Knead trimmings, roll out, and cut additional treats.

Bake until treats are completely dry, about 1½ hours. Let cool on racks.

Charlie Pickles & Pork Chop's Favorite Treat

Pork Chop

{THANKS}

Thanks, everyone.

LORA KIRK—for everything. You are the most talented Chef I know!

KATHLEEN FINLAY—for your beautiful photography and professionalism, and for making sure we did not have to worry about the leftovers.

SASHA SEYMOUR—for food and prop styling. Once again, your sense of humor and spiking of our morning coffees were greatly appreciated!

CHARLOTTE CALON—for your beautiful writing and positive spirit, and for always keeping me on track.

DEB RANKINE—for recipe testing and for being part of the motley crew. I could not have made it without you, Chef!!

STEPHANIE DICKISON—for holding the fort and doing anything and everything at anytime and so much more. Happy Monday!

ALEX LEGGAT—for running errands, dog walking, and falling down the rabbit hole with all of us.

ANDREA MAGYAR—my talented editor, once again. I can't believe you came for seconds. Thank you for this beautiful book!

ALLAN, my brother—for all of your love and support, and for keeping my milk glass always half full of lima beans.

MY STAFF AT RUBY WATCHCO AND RUBY EATS—for all of your support and passion, and for doing what you do so well each and every day!

CHARLIE PICKLES AND PORK CHOP—for keeping the floor tidy. Another batch of cookies is baking!

{INDEX}

salmon
  barbecued, maple mustard, 173
  with mushrooms and sweet corn,
    116–17
salts, flavoured, 167
sauces
  barbecue, 172
  béchamel, 88–91
  caramel, 54, 269
  curry, 118
  jerk barbecue, 177
  Mornay, 44
  parsley pesto, 192
  Romesco, 172
  salted caramel, 291
  tomato basil, 249
sausages
  chorizo, grilled, 191
  chorizo and halibut with clams
    and fennel, 96
  chorizo and potato frittata, 46–47
  and egg bake, 43
  and pork chops, with artichokes
    and rapini, 125
scones
  cranberry, 30
  potato (tattie), 53
seafood
  Bloody Mary shrimp salad, 72
  cioppino, 146
  clams, with chorizo, halibut and
    fennel, 96
  crab risotto, 148–49
  lobster, grilled, 174
  oysters and sirloin steaks, 126
  shrimp with prosciutto, lemon
    and chili, 250
shrimp
  Bloody Mary salad, 72
  with prosciutto, lemon and chili,
    250

smoked salmon
  and caper and dill spread, 20
  chowder, 145
smoothies, 3
soups
  chicken noodle, 140
  cioppino, 146
  French onion, 142
  smoked salmon chowder, 145
  split pea, with ham hocks, 141
sour cream, lemon rosemary, 154
spinach
  and mushroom lasagna, 88–91
spreads
  apple, 21
  bacon cream cheese, 20
  orange mascarpone, 20
  peanut butter, 20
  smoked salmon, caper and dill, 20
  spiced pear, 21
stock
  chicken, 138
  fish, 139
  veal, 139
  vegetable, 138
strawberry
  butter, 17
  and honey jam, 11
  icewine float, 293
  syrup, 51
sweetbreads
  with capers, lemon and brown
    butter, 130
sweet potato
  bourbon cake, 282–83
syrups
  blueberry, 51
  cranberry, 20
  ginger, 224
  lemon, 277
  maple bacon, 51
  peanut butter, 50
  strawberry, 51

T
tempura batter, 260
tomatoes
  and basil sauce, 249
toppings, dessert
  for blueberry buckle, 270
  streusel nut, 27
toppings, salad
  balsamic and basil tomatoes, 64
  brown butter croutons, 64
  candied black olives, 67
  chili orange fried chickpeas, 66
  Espelette-spiced pistachios, 64
  goat cheese thyme frico, 64
  onion rings, 66
  pickled jalapeño peppers, 67
  pickles, 66
  prosciutto crackling, 65
  shaved fennel, 67
trout
  bacon wrapped, with pecan stuffing,
    98–99

V
veal
  chops, 133
  stock, 139
vegetable
  stock, 138

Y
Yorkshire puddings, 221